TEACHING ADULTS
AN ESL RESOURCE BOOK

developed by
Laubach Literacy Action

U.S. Program Division of Laubach Literacy

LAUBACH
LITERACY
ACTION

published by New Readers Press

Acknowledgements

Many people shared in the development and production of this book. They include

- Suzanne Abrams, Linda Church, and Tom Mueller, who did the research, writing, and editing

- Paula Schlusberg, who served as ESL consultant and advisor

- Louise Damen, who contributed many of the ideas shared in "Communicating across Cultures"

- Susan James, who served as project manager and copy editor

- Fran Forstadt, who designed and produced the final materials

Many of the specific activities in the book are adapted from ideas developed by teachers and tutors who have had extensive experience working with ESL learners. Their contributions are acknowledged within the text.

ISBN 1-56420-130-9

Copyright © 1996
New Readers Press
Publishing Division of Laubach Literacy International
Box 131, Syracuse, New York 13210-0131

Printed in the United States of America

Illustrated by Michael Fleishman, Cheri Bladholm, and Fran Forstadt

9 8 7 6 5 4 3

Contents

Introduction

English As a Second Language: The Challenge of Change

Imagine what it would be like to arrive in the United States and be unable to understand, speak, read, or write English. You would not only have to struggle with basic communication, but you would also have to learn to understand the different culture, customs, and behavior of your new neighbors.

The number of people trying to meet this challenge has grown dramatically in recent years. The 1990 U.S. Census indicated that there were five million adults in this country who spoke little or no English. According to the Census, immigrants and refugees accounted for 33–40 percent of the nation's total population growth during the previous 10-year period. Since 1990, approximately one million additional people have entered the United States each year.

The impact of this growth has been especially noticeable in urban areas and among the most disadvantaged populations. The situation is of particular concern to employers who are preparing to meet the needs of a workforce in which increasing numbers of people are classified as "limited English proficient" and in need of English as a Second Language (ESL) instruction.

The ESL population is not only increasing in numbers, but it is also becoming more diversified—in terms of both country of origin and individual skill levels. According to the 1990 Census, the majority of non-native speakers of English in the United States at that time came from Mexico and other Latin American countries. Although they continue to come from these countries, increasing numbers of people are arriving from China, Korea, India, Vietnam, and eastern Europe.

The new arrivals include

- people who come from countries with a strong literacy tradition and who are likely to be literate in their native language

- people who are literate in their native language but are unfamiliar with the Roman alphabet

- people who are unable to read or write in any language because they come from societies that only recently developed a written language or that provide limited educational opportunities

Some of the people who are entering ESL programs will be encountering English for the first time. Others have been in the United States long enough to have acquired some basic listening and speaking skills, but they are unable to read or write the language. Still others studied English in their native countries and are somewhat proficient in reading and writing English but are unable to speak or understand it.

The new arrivals are faced not only with having to learn a new language but also with having to adapt to U.S. culture. For some, that is relatively easy. For others, it can be a major frustration and one that can affect their ability to function effectively both in and out of the classroom.

When you choose to work with ESL learners, you will be confronted with many different needs and challenges. You will also experience the satisfaction of helping people gain the skills and information they need to meet their personal goals. And, if you listen closely, you will discover how much you have touched the lives of these individuals.

One Tutor's Story

Jean-Pierre was the very first ESL learner I worked with after I finished the tutor workshop. He was a 35-year-old carpenter who came to the United States from Haiti seeking political asylum. When I first met him, he could carry on only a rudimentary conversation in English. He had been to school for a few years in Haiti, so he could read and write some French. Haitian Creole was his native language.

Jean-Pierre and I agreed to meet twice a week at the neighborhood library. Although I was nervous at first, we got off to a pretty good start. We seemed to get along quite well. Jean-Pierre's main goal was to learn enough English to start his own business as a carpenter or builder.

One Saturday morning, after we had been meeting for about two weeks, we had a particularly fruitful lesson. We practiced a dialogue and did a follow-up role play to reinforce some language skills we had worked on earlier. By the end of the role play I could tell that

Jean-Pierre was feeling more comfortable with those skills. At his request, we spent the rest of the lesson working on the English he would need to buy some new tools.

After the lesson, as we were walking down the back stairs to leave the library, Jean-Pierre unexpectedly said to me, "When I come this country—afraid. Maybe no learn English. I pray and pray every day. And now—God send you to me."

I was stunned. When I decided to try ESL tutoring, I wasn't really sure what to expect. Now, quite suddenly, the real impact of what I was doing hit home. The training I had gone through, the lesson plans I had worked on, the picture files, the teaching materials, and the activities I was developing; all of this had not prepared me for the most obvious thing: that I would not simply be teaching speaking, listening, reading, and writing in this new role of ESL tutor. I would also be making a profound impact on someone else's life.

This Book

Teaching Adults: An ESL Resource Book was developed to help you meet the needs of people like Jean-Pierre. It includes important background information on language acquisition, adult learning, and cross-cultural issues as well as specific teaching techniques and activities that can be used with a variety of learners.

The material in this book is based on the following principles:

Each adult learner is a unique individual.

Adult learners bring a wealth of knowledge and experience to the learning process. Each learner is a unique individual with his or her own needs and interests. These ideas are at the core of teaching adults. In order to ensure success, the tutor or teacher must work with the learner to tailor the program to the learner's needs, goals, and primary reasons for wanting to learn English.

Instruction must be useful and relevant.

People learn best when they know they will be able to use their new skills and information to meet everyday needs outside the classroom. Because of this, tutors and teachers must utilize teaching activities—such as those included in this book—that incorporate authentic English in real-world contexts. Such activities are a cornerstone of the communicative approach to language instruction. Learners should leave every class with at least one new idea or skill that they can put to immediate use.

Tutoring is effective.

It takes all kinds of programs working together to meet the diverse needs of ESL learners in this country. Volunteer tutors are important partners in that effort. By working in one-to-one or small-group settings, tutors can often provide the individualized attention that may not be available in larger classes. Well-trained tutors assess learner needs, select appropriate instructional materials and activities, and develop lesson plans that help learners reach their goals.

Errors are a natural part of the language learning process.

People learn best when they are encouraged to communicate without worrying about making mistakes. ESL tutors and teachers must create frequent opportunities for learners to share ideas and information as best they can with the English they have learned. During these times, they should allow the learners—especially beginning learners—to concentrate on content and not be overly concerned with grammatical correctness. When a learner makes errors, the tutor or teacher should simply note these and plan to work on them at a later time.

Culture learning is an important part of language learning.

Language is a part of culture. To communicate effectively with English speakers, ESL learners must often learn both a new language and a new culture. Tutors and teachers play an important role as guides to the new culture, helping learners understand the similarities and differences between the culture they encounter in this country and the cultures they bring with them from their native countries. Equipped with this under-standing, the learners will then be able to decide how to blend the two cultures in ways that meet their needs as well as the needs of their families, their employers, and their communities.

Different needs require different solutions.

Because of the diversity among learners, ESL teachers and tutors must be prepared to meet the needs of learners at different levels, from differ-ent cultures, and with a variety of needs and goals. They must be able to assess the learner's needs and then select the teaching approach, techniques, and materials that will meet those needs.

Laubach Literacy Action (LLA) developed this book as one tool to help ESL teachers and tutors respond to the great diversity of learner needs. It is not intended to stand alone but rather to supplement the primary instructional approach or core series being used to teach basic language skills and culture.

Laubach Literacy

Laubach Literacy is a nonprofit, educational corporation that oversees a worldwide network of adult literacy programs and supports research and development aimed at providing effective literacy program models, methods, and materials.

Founded in 1955 by literacy pioneer Frank C. Laubach, the corporation continues to reflect Dr. Laubach's philosophy in its focus:

- to develop instructional materials that are easy to use and culturally appropriate

- to train nonprofessionals, including new readers, as literacy and English as a Second Language (ESL) instructors (consistent with the Laubach motto, "Each One Teach One")

- to publish a variety of audio, video, and print materials that address the needs and interests of the new reader and ESL learner

Laubach Literacy provides financial and technical assistance to community-based programs in Africa, Asia, and Latin America. Each local program is unique because the needs of the learners determine its purpose and the services it provides. Programs are staffed by local people who develop materials specifically for the region they serve.

The work in the United States is carried out through Laubach Literacy Action and New Readers Press.

Laubach Literacy Action

Laubach Literacy Action (LLA) was founded in 1968 to support and promote communication among volunteer organizations that provide literacy and ESL instruction. Its purpose is to enable adults within the United States to acquire the basic level skills in listening, speaking, reading, writing, and mathematics that they need to solve the problems encountered in their daily lives and to participate fully in their society.

LLA works with a wide variety of organizations at local, state, and national levels to provide services to adults in need of basic skills and to advocate for the recognition and support of volunteer tutors and adult literacy programs.

There are more than 1,000 LLA member programs in 46 states. LLA offers technical assistance in all aspects of literacy programming, including program planning, management, evaluation, and tutor training. It also offers optional certification for trainers who conduct tutor workshops. Today there are more than 3,000 LLA-certified trainers in the United States.

LLA works closely with New Readers Press to develop instructional materials, training resources, and volunteer program management materials to help local programs respond to local needs. It provides print and video-based materials that are used to conduct workshops to train volunteer tutors and teachers to work with basic literacy or ESL learners. These workshops build on many of the concepts included in this book. For more information about this training or the other services available from LLA, contact:

> Laubach Literacy Action
> Box 131
> Syracuse, New York 13210-0131
> (315) 422-9121

New Readers Press

New Readers Press (NRP), Laubach Literacy's U.S. publishing division, has been providing educational materials to literacy and ESL programs since 1967. NRP develops, publishes, and distributes print, audio, video, and computer-based instructional materials that help adults and young adults acquire the basic reading, writing, listening, speaking, and mathematical skills they need to survive in today's complex society. NRP products are available from the basic skills level through the GED level. (See Appendix A for a list of some of the products used in ESL instruction.) To request a copy of the NRP catalog, contact:

> New Readers Press
> Department TBDE
> P.O. Box 888
> Syracuse, New York 13210-0888
> (800) 448-8878

Language Learning

The Four Basic Language Skills

One definition of "language" is *a system of symbols that permit people to communicate or interact. These symbols can include vocal and written forms, gestures, and body language.*

Another way to describe language is in terms of the four basic language skills: listening, speaking, reading, and writing. In your teaching, you will need to address each of these skills. And, whenever possible, you should utilize activities that integrate all four skills since each reinforces the other.

People generally learn these four skills in the following order:

Listening: When people are learning a new language (or, in the case of children, their first language), they first hear it spoken.

Speaking: Eventually, they try to repeat what they hear.

Reading: Later, they see the spoken language depicted symbolically in print.

Writing: Finally, they reproduce these symbols on paper.

Implications for teaching

1. Understand that a person first learns to speak by listening. Make sure that the learners have plenty of opportunity to listen to and understand the spoken language.

2. Set up activities in which the learners practice speaking by using language they have already heard and understood.

3. Always introduce something new orally before asking learners to read it.

4. Always try to create a context that ensures the learner will understand what he or she is saying. For example, you might decide to teach the sentence *He is running*. Instead of simply saying it and asking the learner to repeat it, you can provide a context by running across the room or showing a picture of a child running. This is especially important with learners who are very good at mimicking the sounds of English and who may be able to repeat the words and sentences they hear almost perfectly without understanding anything the speaker is saying.

5. Try to relate the new language to the individual learner's current language ability as well as his or her previous knowledge and experience. For example, if a learner plays a lot of baseball, you can show a picture of a person running to first base to teach the sentence *He is running*. However, such a picture might be totally inappropriate for a learner who has never seen or played baseball.

The Functions of Language

As you think about how to address each of the four language skills, you should also keep in mind that every time people use language, they do so for a particular purpose or function. Examples include

greeting	parting	inviting	accepting
making excuses	requesting	interrupting	complaining
arguing	complimenting	congratulating	flattering
seducing	evading	lying	shifting blame
changing the subject	criticizing	reprimanding	ridiculing
insulting	warning	accusing	denying
agreeing	disagreeing	apologizing	persuading
insisting	suggesting	reminding	asserting
reporting	evaluating	commenting	advising
sympathizing	commanding	ordering	demanding
questioning	probing		

Each of these functions has specific language associated with it. To communicate successfully, people need to learn the appropriate language to carry out each function. For example, you might teach some of the following phrases if you want to teach about *inviting:*

> *Would you like to . . . ?*
> *How would you like to . . . ?*
> *How about . . . ?*
> *I'd be pleased if you would . . .*

Second Language Acquisition

In your work as an ESL tutor or teacher, keep in mind that no two learners are alike. Three important areas of difference are the following:

1. Language skill level

   - Some learners will speak some English, but not be able to read or write it.

   - Some will be able to read and write English, but not speak it.

   - Some will not be able to read and write in their first language.

   - Some will have a first language that does not use the Roman alphabet (e.g., Russian, Arabic, or Thai).

2. Degree of comfort when trying to speak a new language

   - Some learners are not at all shy about "blurting out" something in English, and they are not overly concerned about perfect grammar or pronunciation.

   - Some become embarrassed if they think they are making too many mistakes.

   - Some think they shouldn't say anything at all unless their English is perfect.

3. Learning rate

   - Some people can learn a language quickly; others simply don't have a strong "knack" for picking up languages.

   - Learners who have a lot of contact with English speakers usually progress faster than those who don't.

Because of these differences, no single teaching approach or set of materials can meet the needs of all learners—or even all the needs of a single learner. As a tutor, you will have to continually make decisions about

- which ESL activities and materials to use

- how to motivate learners to seek out and communicate with English speakers other than yourself

- how to create an effective atmosphere for language learning

You can make such decisions effectively if you understand the process of second language acquisition—that is, what happens when someone is learning a new language. Inherent in the process of learning a new language are the four principles discussed on pp. 16–20.

Principle #1: Meaningful Communication

> Language learners are more highly motivated when the communication in which they are involved is meaningful to them.

People learning a second language want to learn to say, understand, read, and write those things that will be of real and immediate use to them. When they know they can use what they learn, they are more apt to remember it.

As they experience success in using English to communicate in the outside world, learners will come to ESL class with more and more self-confidence and enthusiasm: "Hey, I really *am* learning English! I ordered a hamburger today without just pointing to the picture on the menu. I told the waitress what I wanted and she took my order!"

Implications for teaching

1. Use ESL activities and exercises that have a real purpose to them. One way to do this is to ensure that the activities you choose include an "information gap." An information gap activity requires learners to share information in order to complete a *real* communication task. For examples, see Activities #58–59.

2. Teach learners the things *they* want to learn. Find out what their goals are and teach the skills they need to meet them.

3. Use examples in class that draw from the learners' own lives.

4. Set up role plays that are similar to actual situations where the learners will have to use English. For an example, see Activity #15.

Principle #2: Success, Not Perfection

> The ESL learner is usually more concerned about being able to communicate successfully than about being correct.

The important thing for most beginning-level language learners is successful communication—not whether the language they use is correct. These learners are not focusing on grammar or pronunciation issues, but on meeting their basic everyday needs such as asking directions or mailing a package at the post office. Their situation is similar to that of a child who is learning to speak. The child successfully communicates the fact that he or she is thirsty by saying the word *juice*. Neither the child nor the mother is concerned at this stage with the child's inability to correctly say, "May I have a cup of juice, please?"

Tutors and teachers need to celebrate the beginning learners' successes and not focus on their errors. In the story below, an ESL tutor describes his experience with a learner from Vietnam.

"Me No Go Work"

A couple of years ago I was tutoring Canh, a beginning-level ESL learner who could barely get by in English. He worked as a custodian at an elementary school. I had been meeting with him twice a week for about three months.

During an ESL lesson on the day after Columbus Day, I asked Canh if he had gone to work the day before. He answered, "Me no go work yesterday."

I was delighted! Canh had used English to answer my question successfully! By his response, I understood that he had not worked yesterday. As his tutor, I wasn't concerned that he said "me" instead of "I." He got the pronoun in the correct place—at the beginning of the sentence.

Not only that, Canh used a negative. He did say "no" instead of "not," but at his stage of English language development, that's OK. He got his idea across!

Implications for teaching

1. Be patient and understand that a beginning ESL learner moves from zero ability to near-native fluency in stages clearly marked by a gradual progression from imprecise to accurate levels of English. Allow the learner to move through each of these stages.

2. Encourage the learner to try to communicate in English at every stage, no matter how imprecisely. The very act of communicating is an essential part of the learning process and prepares the learner to advance to the next stage.

3. Recognize that comprehension always precedes production. Beginning language learners can understand much more of the new language than they are able to speak. They build from there. This is as true for adults learning a second language as it is for children learning their first language. Don't think that simply because a learner makes a lot of errors when speaking that he or she won't be able to understand you.

4. Focus on teaching the learners how to use the language to create meaning rather than on how the language works (the grammar or rules).

5. Resist the temptation to constantly correct learners when they make mistakes. Keep in mind the following points about error correction:

   • Correct learners if you really do not understand what they are saying.

   • Correct learners when you are trying to teach a specific way of saying something. For example, if you are teaching learners to make a request by using the new phrase *I would like . . .* , you will want to make sure learners are able to say the phrase correctly.

   • Do not correct learners during activities such as role plays that are designed to encourage the learner to concentrate on communicating for meaning. Let learners use whatever English they have at their disposal to get their ideas across.

6. Understand that trying to correct beginning learners can cause confusion. For example, if the tutor in the story above had tried to correct Canh, the results might have been the following:

Tutor:	Canh, did you have to go to work yesterday?
Canh:	Me no go work yesterday.
Tutor:	*I didn't* go to work yesterday.
Canh:	Oh! You, too, teacher?

Principle #3: Anxiety

> Learners are more successful at acquiring language when their anxiety level is low.

This principle applies to learning anything—not just another language. People seem to be able to learn best when

• they are relaxed

• they know it's OK to make mistakes

• they are reassured that, overall, they are doing well

Implications for teaching

1. Have fun with learners, and allow *them* to have fun, too.

2. Select classroom activities in which learners can feel some degree of success. A good example is Total Physical Response (see Activity #3), which allows learners to listen and respond without having to speak.

3. Begin each session with something the learners can do well.

4. Don't test learners or put them on the spot during the course of conversation or oral activities. Risk is already involved when people are trying out new language forms, so the learner's anxiety level should be kept to a minimum wherever possible.

Principle #4: Exposure

> Progress in a second language depends in part on the amount of exposure to speakers of that language.

To move beyond a very basic language ability, people must

- have an immediate opportunity to use the language they are studying

- be in a position where they won't get some of their basic needs met unless they can communicate in that language

Some ESL learners have little contact with speakers of English apart from their tutors and classmates. Classroom practice might amount to only a few hours per week. As a result, many learners reach a plateau, and their progress stops. That's because they are having their most important social needs met in their first language. They are using their first language to discuss such things as family affairs, politics, personal desires, and plans for the future. Such issues are closest to them, and require complex language for articulating opinions and feelings.

These learners probably use English only for such basic tasks as asking directions, ordering food, cashing their paychecks, or doing jobs that require only a limited number of stock phrases.

Implications for teaching

1. Devise ways to motivate learners to speak about more than superficial things.

2. Encourage and motivate learners to have more contact with other speakers of English.

3. Encourage learners to identify specific things they want to be able to say or do that require better English skills. For example, if a learner wants to buy a car, you could

   - teach the learner to read the classified ads

   - do role plays to practice contacting a used-car owner

   - help the learner make several calls to car owners

4. Organize role plays and field trips to help prepare learners to be "out there" on their own with English speakers.

The principles described above are consistent with a communicative approach to teaching ESL—an approach that focuses on enabling people to use the language to communicate with English speakers to meet their own needs.

Communicating across Cultures

Culture represents the ways and means by which human beings deal with universal human situations and problems using a variety of culture-specific patterns related to values, beliefs, and behaviors in a given social group.

Culture includes all those things that make up our daily lives. It includes social relations, religion, art, beliefs, values, clothes, food, marriage, child rearing, family, education, entertainment, clothing, housing, work, and laws.

When people share the same culture, they don't have to spend a lot of time agonizing over what to do or how to act appropriately. Their "cultural map" helps them decide what type of clothes to wear, what side of the street to drive on, and whether to bow or shake hands when meeting someone.

But ESL learners who are new to this country will not have the U.S. cultural map at their disposal. Instead, they will constantly have to be thinking about what to do, even in the apparently simplest social situations. Some will just carry out their daily activities according to the same cultural map they have used all their lives—thus running the risk of doing culturally inappropriate things or being misjudged.

As a tutor, you will not only be teaching a new language, but you will be helping the learner use that language in a new culture. You will be acting as a guide to the American culture. (Note that the term *American* is used in this section to refer to people who live in the United States or to cultural attitudes and behaviors that are seen as typical of people in this country.)

(Louise Damen contributed much of the material used in whole or in part in this section.)

Language Learning and Culture Learning

The diagram below represents the relationship between a second language learner's first language and culture and the new language and culture.

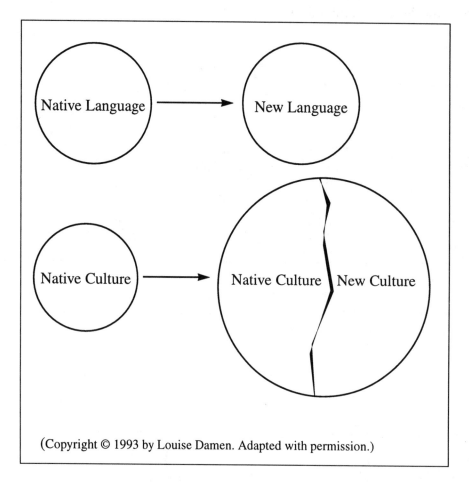

(Copyright © 1993 by Louise Damen. Adapted with permission.)

Language learning means replacing one language with a new language. The learner has little or no freedom to mix and match. Exceptions occur when a learner retains words that have no English substitute, such as words for native foods.

On the other hand, *culture learning* is a selective or combining process in which the learner decides which elements of the native culture to retain and which elements of the new culture to adapt or adopt. The learner's new cultural identity will represent a *mixture* of the native culture and the new culture. For example, a learner may adopt a new way of greeting someone (handshake instead of bow) but maintain the old rule of avoiding eye contact. Each learner will differ in how much of the new culture he or she chooses to adopt.

Individual Responses to Universal Situations

People of all cultures face the same universal problems or situations, but the cultural responses—the specific ways in which individual cultures handle these situations—can be quite different. The following chart illustrates how this might work for three different universal situations.

Cultural Elements		
Universal	**Culture-Specific**	
	Non-U.S.	**U.S.**
Child rearing	• extended family: everyone (not just the parents) helps out with children (Indonesia, Mexico) • delay in naming newborn child (India)	• nuclear family • often done before birth
Eating/Food	• chopsticks (China, Japan) • spicy/hot (India) • 3rd meal very late at night (Spain)	• knife/fork • generally not spicy • early evening
Marriage	• arranged; family approves (Middle and Far East)	• personal choice

It is important to understand that not all learners will need help with learning U.S. cultural responses. As a tutor, you should simply be alert to areas in which there are likely to be cross-cultural differences.

The following are three examples of possible cultural differences. As you read them, remember that there is no "best" or "only" response to a universal situation. It is often difficult, however, to accept someone else's ways as valid because our own cultural ways are so ingrained in us.

Time

Some cultures have different attitudes toward time and punctuality from what is usual in the American culture. For example, a learner may consistently drift in late for an ESL session. When this happens, it may be because he or she simply is not accustomed to thinking in terms of exact time and keeping appointments. Whether or not you personally have a problem with learners who are late to class, you have an obligation to help people understand how others in this country might react to or judge a person who is chronically late.

Some specific things that you can do as a tutor in this situation include the following:

- Tell the learner that you have only a limited amount of time. The class begins at a certain time and ends at a certain time. If necessary because of limited English ability, use a clock to show the learner the starting time and ending time. Explain that you must leave when the class ends. Stick to those beginning and ending times for your class sessions.

- If you are teaching a small group or class, tell the learner that you always start the session on time to be fair to the other learners. Explain that arriving late is disruptive to the other learners who do arrive on time and that people might miss something important if they arrive late.

- Tell the learner that getting and keeping a job in this country depends in part on a person's ability to be "on time." (You will also have to clearly define "on time," which can mean different things in different U.S. settings. For example, in some jobs, a person scheduled to start work at 9:00 could be considered "on time" if he or she arrived at 8:50 or 9:10. However, someone planning to go to a movie must understand that "on time" generally means the exact time stated in the newspaper.)

Attitudes toward Teachers

Adult learners from some cultures may have unexpected attitudes toward teachers and tutors. You should be aware of these as you teach. The following are some examples:

- In some cultures, a teacher is revered as a special person—someone who deserves a particularly high level of respect. Learners from these cultures (such as China, Japan, or Vietnam) may balk at addressing a tutor or teacher by first name, even when requested to do so. Be understanding if a learner prefers to use *Mr., Mrs.,* or even *Teacher* in addressing you. (The latter is a mark of respect. It is not considered a childish term as it is in the United States.)

- Although you want to encourage learners to think on their own and to be critical in their analysis of new information, learners from some cultures (such as Japan) may find it difficult to question you or to take risks in the learning situation. In their prior school experiences, such learners may have been expected to play a more passive role, simply taking in information without ever initiating any interaction with the teacher.

- Some learners may not want to be seen as the center of attention. In Japan, for example, there is a saying: "The nail that sticks up gets hammered down." Such learners may not feel comfortable taking part in role plays.

- Asking some learners what they want to learn (consistent with a learner-centered approach) might cause them to question your ability since, in their eyes, you do not seem to know what you are supposed to teach. In such cases, you should refer to the needs assessment done when the learner entered the program to determine the most appropriate content or teaching methods.

- Learners from some cultures (such as Saudi Arabia and other Muslim countries) may be uncomfortable learning in a class with members of the opposite sex since male and female students are usually separated after a certain grade in school.

Eye Contact

In the United States, making eye contact with someone can indicate that we are interested in what the speaker is saying or that we are sincere about what we ourselves are saying. A speaker who does not make eye contact can seem shifty or even dishonest. (On the other hand, too much eye contact can be interpreted as staring or being rude.)

But learners from some cultures (such as Cambodia or Vietnam) may be reluctant to make eye contact with the teacher. They have been brought up to believe that it is disrespectful to look the teacher (or other person in authority) in the eye.

Although the amount of eye contact may not cause a problem in the teaching situation itself, you should find a way to discuss it with the learners. For example, if you are talking about interviewing for a job, you can explain that not looking someone in the eye might be interpreted as a sign of dishonesty in the United States. Or, in some cases, it may imply a lack of confidence in one's own abilities. In creating job-related role plays, you should find a way to help such learners practice making eye contact with the (prospective) boss.

Being an Effective Culture Guide

In your role of culture guide, you are helping the learners discover how the American culture "works." Together, you and the learners will be developing an awareness of each other's culture—both the differences and the similarities. Enjoy the process!

The tips on pp. 26–27 are useful when thinking about culture and your role as a tutor and guide.

Tips on Being an Effective Culture Guide

1. **Recognize who you are as a culture guide (examples: age, gender, life experience, personal likes and dislikes, etc.).**

   You are an American, but also a specific American with your own individual cultural roles and experiences. Never pose as the only "real" American. Your own view may be going out of style. By the same token, the learners do not represent *all* people from their culture. Each person is unique. Avoid stereotyping.

2. **Learn as much about the learner's culture as you teach about your own.**

   This helps the learner by reinforcing his or her own cultural identity as valid, and it helps you discover points of contrast. An easy way to learn about culture is to ask questions of each other and discuss the answers. "What is a friend in your country?" "What's the best way to find a job in your country?" "What do you like about the United States? What don't you like?" In this way, teacher and learner function as mutual culture guides/informants.

3. **Examine similarities between the cultures as well as differences.**

   Similarities bind us together. Differences help us see the many ways we solve universal problems. Both are important. Learn to value the similarities and respect the differences.

4. **Explore cultural meanings found in words, phrases, and gestures.**

   Examples: In the United States, there is a difference between referring to someone as "fat" and "overweight." The side-to-side head shake is not a universal way to say "no." Nor does the "OK" sign with the thumb to forefinger mean the same in every culture. Colors, too, carry meanings that can vary across cultures. White is not always for the bride, and yellow doesn't always signify a coward.

5. **Encourage the learner to practice guessing what is or is not appropriate in the new culture.**

   Examples: When are gifts expected? What is the right time to arrive for a dinner party? How does one decline a party invitation? What do Americans mean when they say, "See you later"?

6. **Train yourself and the learner to be prepared for expressions that are not meant to be taken literally, or that have culture-specific meanings.**

   For instance, the expression "Let's have lunch sometime" does not necessarily mean that the speaker is inviting the listener to lunch. In fact, it's not likely to mean that at all. Such lunch invitations are most often mere expressions of politeness on a par with the standard "How are you?"

(Copyright © 1993 by Louise Damen. Adapted with permission.)

Culture guide continued ▶

7. **Take time to explore the learner's perceptions and conclusions by f‹
   ing up with an observation of your own, or a question.**

   When the learner describes a situation he or she encounters, you could ask,
   "What does that mean to you?" or "What did you see going on?" Discussing
   an event with cultural overtones from the learner's life helps bring clarity
   about cultural issues.

8. **Avoid being judgmental of either yourself or the learner.**

   As you build mutual trust, you and the learner will realize it's OK to make
   mistakes in your interpretations of each other's cultural behaviors.

9. **Realize that forming a new identity in a new cultural setting is a matter of
   "learner's choice."**

   You can set objectives for what you want to teach about culture. But the
   learners must be the ones to decide which parts of the new culture to adapt
   or adopt. One's cultural identity is a personal work of art.

10. **Be aware that learners often experience major adjustment problems.**

    Be supportive, but do not undertake major therapy. Your role is simply to
    facilitate cultural adjustment as best you can.

Activity 1

Culture: Critical Incidents

Purpose

To enable ESL learners to engage in a discussion about a specific incident to
understand what the appropriate response might be in the American culture

How

1. Select a social situation in which you have noticed that people from other
   cultures often fail to respond appropriately—a situation in which the person new to the culture and the American might be surprised or confused
   by each other's behavior. Example: situations related to time.

2. Write a critical incident—a scenario related to this situation. Create three
   or four possible choices for how a person should respond in that situation.

If possible, make one of the choices a response that would be appropriate in the learner's own culture. Example of a critical incident related to time:

Betty asked Maria to dinner and told her to come around 6:00 p.m. When should Maria arrive?

    a. anytime convenient
    b. 10 minutes before 6:00
    c. 10 minutes after 6:00
    d. precisely at 6:00

(Copyright © 1993 by Louise Damen. Adapted with permission.)

3. Give each learner a copy of the critical incident.

4. Ask each learner to read the incident and choose the answer he or she thinks is most appropriate.

5. Review each response one at a time. Invite participants to discuss the consequences of each and why they chose the one they did. Examples of what they might say about the critical incident described above:

   • *a* would be rude because Betty would be unable to plan and would have no idea when to have the meal ready

   • *b* would be inconsiderate since Betty might not be ready yet and would prefer to have everything prepared before her guest arrives

   • *c* is probably the safest choice

   • *d* would probably be fine, but it might be good to give Betty just a few extra minutes to finish preparations or just relax before her company arrives

6. Invite the learners to discuss their own attitudes toward time and what they have learned about American attitudes toward time. Your goal will be to help them understand what might be the most appropriate course of action for the American culture.

Suggestions

• Learners from different cultural backgrounds may come up with a variety of reasons for arriving at a particular time. Your main job will be to allow the discussion to flow and enable people to share many different ideas. Then you can work on helping learners understand appropriate behavior in American culture.

• It is important to discuss each choice rather than just ask "What is the correct choice?" You want to have the learners consider the consequences of each possibility within U.S. culture.

- Be aware of the following before you try the critical incident about when to arrive for dinner: In the United States, the safest choice is probably *c*, but not all Americans would agree on this. A lack of consensus could be a reflection of the fact that we are all independent culture learners—and that there are many subcultures within any culture. Cultures are always changing, so there is room for debate and divergent answers.

- Other examples of critical incidents:

You are a guest for the evening in an American home. At about 10:00 p.m., the hostess begins cleaning up. What should you do?

    a. Get up and start washing the dishes.

    b. Say good night and leave at once.

    c. Help her carry out the dishes and then say it's time for you to leave.

An American friend tells you, "Drop by some Sunday." When you do so the next Sunday, he seems surprised and upset. What is going on?

    a. He was just being friendly when he invited you. He didn't really expect you to visit.

    b. You chose the wrong Sunday.

    c. You should have called before visiting.

Activity 2

Newspapers As a Cultural Key

Purpose

To use the newspaper classified ads as a way to create a discussion of different cross-cultural behaviors

How

1. In advance, save copies of the classified ads in your local paper. You will need one set of ads for each person, but they do not have to be from the same day's paper.

2. Highlight the section headings on each learner's copy.

3. The learners will work in groups of three. For each group, you will need to prepare a different card related to one of the section headings. Put the section heading on the front of the card. On the back, write questions designed to stimulate discussion about cultural issues related to that section. Examples:

"Merchandise"

In your country:

- Do people advertise things for sale in the newspaper?

- If so, is there a fixed price, or do people bargain?

Do Americans bargain?

"Roommates"

In your country:

- Do strangers share apartments?

- Do young men and women live on their own before they get married?

What do you think about some Americans who live away from their families before they are married?

"Employment"

In your country:

- Do employers advertise their jobs in the paper?

- Do people usually get jobs by knowing someone important?

How do you think Americans find jobs?

"Pets"

> In your country:
>
> - Do people buy and sell pets?
>
> - What are some common pets in your country?
>
> What do you think about Americans and their pets?

4. Give each group one of the cards and three copies of the classified ads.

5. Ask each group to do the following:

   a. Look for the section of the classified ads that matches the name on the front of the card.

   b. Read some of the ads under that heading to each other.

   c. Discuss the questions on the back of the card.

6. After the groups have had a chance to complete their discussions, call on each group to report what they discussed. Open the discussion to the rest of the class. After a minute or two of follow-up discussion, clarify for everyone the way Americans might handle any of the issues that have come up.

Suggestions

- If possible, try to mix learners from different countries in each of the small groups. This will make for more interesting discussion.

- You can also do this activity with the whole group rather than with small groups. Read the card to the group and then let them discuss the questions. You can then repeat the activity in different lessons, using one card each time.

- Other sections of the newspaper can also be used to point out and discuss American cultural behavior. Examples: personal advice columns, store advertisements, or the comics.

Finding Out about the Learners

There are two types of ESL learner assessment: needs assessment and skills assessment. Together, these create a highly useful, multi-dimensional profile of the learner. You will add to this profile as you and the learner work together over time and you get to know more about the learner. The information you gather from these two assessments will help you

- identify the learner's changing needs, interests, goals, and English abilities

- make decisions about which skills the learner needs to work on, and which topics, teaching techniques, and materials are appropriate for that learner

- tailor teaching materials to the learner

For a sample of an initial profile done on a new learner, see p. 158.

Needs Assessment

A needs assessment identifies the learner's background, interests, goals, and immediate needs. This knowledge will help you determine what information and skills the learner will need, as well as what materials and activities to use. Examples of questions to ask during a needs assessment:

Sample Needs Assessment Inventory	
1. **Name**	*I'm your tutor, [Name]. What is your name?*
2. **Homeland**	*Where are you from? Tell me about your country.*
3. **How long in United States**	*How long have you been in the United States?*
4. **Family**	*Tell me about your family. What are your children's names? How old are they?*

Needs assessment continued ▶

5. **Job in United States**	*What do you do at work? How long have you worked there? What do you like about your job?*
6. **Work experience in homeland**	*What kind of work did you do in [Homeland]? For how long? Did you like your work?*
7. **Education**	*Did you go to school in [Homeland]? How many years did you go to school?*
8. **Personal interests**	*What do you like to do when you are not in school or working? What did you do last weekend?*
9. **Goals**	*What are your short- and long-term goals for your life? What would you like to do in the next 5 years? 10 years?*
10. **Reasons for learning English**	*Why do you want to learn English? What do you want to be able to do that you can't do now? How will English help you reach your goals?*

Don't expect to complete the needs assessment inventory in one meeting. Many of the questions will be answered as you get to know the learner better.

Skills Assessment

A skills assessment shows the learner's current English-language listening, speaking, reading, and writing abilities. Skills assessments may be done at three different points:

- as part of the intake process: to find out what the learner's skills are upon entering the program

- periodically during the learning: to measure the learner's progress

- when the learner leaves the program: to measure progress and to determine appropriate referrals for additional assistance if necessary

ESL programs use many different methods to assess learners' skills. (For a description of two assessment tools, see Appendix C.) You can also do your own informal assessment to help answer the following basic questions:

Teaching Adults: An ESL Resource Book

	Sample Skills Assessment
Comprehension	Does the learner understand anything at all that you say? Does the learner understand simple commands or directions? Does the learner ask you—or gesture for you—to repeat?
Speaking	Is the learner's speech intelligible, or do you have to keep asking the learner to repeat?
	Is the learner's speech fluent? That is, can the learner maintain a flow of understandable speech, whether or not it is grammatically accurate?
	Does the learner pronounce individual sounds reasonably well?
	Is the learner's intonation pattern at all close to that of American English?
	Does the learner speak with any degree of grammatical accuracy?
Reading	Can the learner read his or her name? Can the learner read simple signs?
Writing	Can the learner hold a pen or pencil properly?
	Can the learner print or write his or her own name using the Roman (English) alphabet?
	Can the learner fill in blanks on a form?

The activities described below will help you get this information.

"Hello, how are you?"

When you meet the learner for the first time, use a basic, everyday greeting such as "Hello, how are you?" If the learner says nothing and has a blank look, it probably means that he or she is not able to understand the greeting. Since basic greetings are always introduced in beginning-level ESL classes, you could assume that overall the learner understands very little oral English.

If the learner responds with something like "Fine, thank you," note the accuracy of his or her pronunciation. Is it close to native English pronunciation? Does the learner have good pronunciation of individual sounds, but not the appropriate intonation pattern?

If the learner responds with something like "Me good," he or she is probably a beginning-level learner with some exposure to English.

"My name is _____. What's your name?"

Asking this question will give you additional information about the learner's skills. Does the learner make some attempt to provide his or her name?

"Read your name."

Have two name tags ready, one with your name printed on it and one with the learner's name. Point to your name tag and say, "My name is _____." Hand the other name tag to the learner. Point to it and ask, "Please read." If the learner looks confused, point again and draw your finger along the name. Give the learner time to respond.

"Write your name."

Ask the learner to write his or her name. If necessary, point to your own name tag. Say, "My name is _____." Print your name on a piece of paper as you repeat, "My name is_____." Then ask the learner to do the same. Keep in mind that the learner might be able to write his or her name, but not be able to understand your request.

"Follow the directions."

Be prepared with a series of tasks that require only physical (not oral) responses. Examples: "Please give me the_____." "Come with me." "Please sit here." (See "Total Physical Response" on pp. 40–46.) Note how well the learner is able to carry out the requests.

"Talk about the picture."

Ask the learner a series of questions about a picture you bring to class. Start with easy questions. Then go on to more difficult ones. For examples, see Activity #21.

Keep the following tips in mind whenever you do a skills assessment:

• Give the learner time to respond. Silence does not mean that nothing is happening. The learner may need time to think.

• Remember that most learners understand more than they can say. This is a normal stage of development, so don't assume that the learner has some unusual problem with his or her speaking skills. (The same applies to learners who seem to read better than they can write.)

Listening and Speaking

When tutoring beginning-level ESL learners, always start with the oral language skills of listening and speaking. Those are the skills that will most quickly and directly aid beginning learners in their daily lives.

The activities in this section are intended for use with beginning-level learners, but you can easily adapt them for learners at all levels. More advanced learners also need to work on their oral skills to improve their ability to understand spoken English and produce English conversation.

Guidelines for Teaching Oral Skills

The following are some helpful guidelines to keep in mind when teaching oral skills:

1. Don't worry about not being able to communicate with the learners—even when they don't know a word of English. You will not have to be able to speak their language to teach them effectively. Total Physical Response, described on pp. 40–46, is an ideal teaching technique to use with learners who are at this basic level.

2. Use gestures to indicate when the learners should listen, speak, or stop speaking. These gestures are especially important to use with beginning learners and will help the initial lessons go much more smoothly. In time, the learner will understand what to do. Then you will only need to use gestures when introducing a new drill or exercise.

Listen

Put one finger up to your lips in a "shhh" gesture and the other hand behind your ear. This means the learner should listen to you and not talk.

Stop

Raise your hand no higher than your shoulder, palm facing the learner. The stop gesture means "It's time for me to speak now." For example, you can use this gesture when the learner finishes a line of the dialogue and you are going to give the next line.

Beckon

Extend your arm, palm up. Then pull up hand and forearm toward you. The beckon gesture means "Go ahead and speak."

3. You can either "mouth" or whisper the learner's lines to help him or her get started. Mouthing or whispering establishes that the line is the learner's line, not yours. For example, when you are practicing a dialogue, the learner may not be able to remember the next line. In this case, simply begin to mouth or whisper it, and use the beckon gesture to encourage the learner to repeat it aloud.

4. Focus on teaching the words, phrases, and grammatical structures that learners must have to meet their everyday needs. Examples of such needs might be applying for a job, renting an apartment, or buying groceries. Your goal is to enable learners to take what they have just learned in the classroom and use it immediately in the outside world.

5. Use objects or pictures to illustrate the meaning of words or help learners understand the context for an activity. For example, when doing a role play about making a bank deposit, you could use checks, deposit slips, personal identification, and a picture of the inside of a bank.

In choosing pictures, look for those that are large enough for everyone in the group to see, that show people engaged in activities likely to generate conversation, and that represent a variety of ethnic, economic, and age groups. Pictures that reflect the learners' personal interests are also a big plus.

Select your pictures to meet your teaching needs. For example, pictures of single objects can be used to teach vocabulary or grammar. Pictures showing a sequence can be used to demonstrate steps in a process, such as changing a tire or tying a necktie. Pictures that have a lot of elements and action have a wide variety of applications. You can ask learners to describe what is happening in such pictures, or to imagine what the people in the picture are thinking.

One of the first things to do as a tutor is to start developing your own picture file. Magazines and newspapers are excellent sources. To make the file most useful, divide the pictures into categories. Examples:

- animals

- clothing

- foods (This category can be broken down into smaller categories such as fruits, vegetables, desserts.)

- occupations

- opposites *(big/small, tall/short, happy/sad)*

- sports

- unusual things (great as conversation starters)

- grammar or structures (Pictures can be used to teach things like action verbs, *running,* or modal auxiliaries, *must be.* Example of the latter: a picture of a cityscape with the Statue of Liberty to teach "This *must be* New York." See Activity #12.)

6. Do not assume that learners don't understand a word or phrase just because they are unable to say it or are reluctant to try. Since comprehension precedes production, even beginning learners are able to understand more than they can say themselves. But they need to start speaking as much as possible in order to improve.

7. Remember that learners will make lots of errors as they are learning to speak English. This is a natural stage in the learning process. It doesn't mean that learners are not making progress or that you are doing a poor job of teaching.

8. Make corrections only at the appropriate times. For example, it would not be appropriate to interrupt a role play to correct a learner's grammar or pronunciation. This is a time when the learner's goal is to express ideas, not to speak with perfection.

9. Be patient. Give learners plenty of time to respond to your questions or requests. Learn to be comfortable with silence while learners are thinking about what to say or how to say it.

Introducing New Vocabulary

The first step in teaching oral skills is to help the learner acquire a basic vocabulary of useful words and phrases. Keep in mind the following guidelines when you are teaching vocabulary:

1. Teach only a few new words (four to six maximum) at a time.

2. With beginning learners, choose one way of saying something and stick with it. For example, if you teach the expression "Turn off the light," don't give other versions of the same expression ("Switch off the light," "Turn out the light," or "Put out the light").

3. Use repetition. To make new words a permanent part of their vocabulary, learners need to hear and use them over and over again. Your teaching routine should include recycling of new words in later lessons.

4. If you want to teach learners a new word by showing an object or picture, show multiple examples of the object or picture. That way, there is no danger that the learners will misunderstand what the word means. For example, to teach the word *pencil*, show learners three different types of pencils. If you use only one, learners might think that you are teaching the word *yellow, straight,* or *write*.

Total Physical Response

Total Physical Response (TPR) is a teaching technique that enables learners to acquire new English vocabulary by listening to and carrying out spoken commands. In TPR activities, learners are not required to speak. The tutor models the commands and continually repeats and reviews them until the learners can carry out the commands with no difficulty. Learners are more likely to be and feel successful when the tutor provides constant support and modeling and eliminates the pressure on learners to speak the new words.

Although TPR can be used with learners at all levels, it is most useful with those who understand little or no English. At this level, gestures and facial expressions are especially important.

With beginning learners, first teach basic commands that call for simple body movements and no props: *stand up, sit down, walk,* and *turn around.* (See Activity #4.) This gives learners a welcome feeling of accomplishment and helps them become comfortable with TPR right away.

Learners can go on to more advanced TPR activities in which they interact with props and people in the learning environment. Examples of commands to use at this stage are *touch the, point to, pick up, put down,* and *give me.* These are especially useful for teaching the names of both objects in pictures and of objects that are in the immediate environment, some of which may be out of reach.

You can also use TPR for the following purposes:

- to review and reinforce vocabulary you have already taught using non-TPR methods

- as a "catch-up" at the beginning of a lesson for the benefit of learners who have missed previous lessons in which new material was introduced

- to provide learners with an enjoyable, relaxing break during a lesson

All TPR activities have the four basic steps shown below. These are more fully described in Activity #3.

Steps in Using TPR

1. Do the action as you give the new command.

2. Do the action with the learner several times as you give the command.

3. Give the command without doing the action yourself.

4. Do the action again if the learner has difficulty carrying out the command.

Activity

3 Total Physical Response (TPR)—Basic Steps

Purpose

To give learners an opportunity to hear and understand English words and phrases without having to produce them

How

1. Select the commands (and vocabulary) you are going to teach.

2. Before the teaching session, make a list of the complete commands in the order you plan to teach them.

   (The list will serve as a record of what you have taught and will help you plan review activities for later lessons. Lists are also important when working with more advanced learners who will be learning longer and more complex commands. The list will enable you to repeat your exact instructions in case a learner asks you to do so.)

3. Gather any equipment, props, or pictures you will need to set the context or illustrate the meaning of the commands.

   (If you will be teaching commands that involve objects, bring to the lesson two examples of each object. This will allow you to model the command using one object and to have the learner use the other object to carry out the command at the same time.)

4. If you are working with a group, select two or three learners for the demonstration.

   (Teaching more than one learner at the same time takes the pressure off any individual learner. The other learners in the class will also be learning as they watch. When you finish the demonstration, you can invite other learners to carry out the commands they saw you teach.)

5. Teach the commands.

   a. Model the action as you give the first command. As you do this, use gestures and facial expressions to help the learners understand what you want them to do.

   b. Do the action with the learners several times, and give the command each time you do the action.

      (If you are teaching the English words for objects, you will need to work with only one learner at a time as the others watch—unless you have enough objects for more than one learner.)

   c. Give the command without doing the action yourself.

   d. If the learners have difficulty carrying out the command, model the action again as you say the command. Always be ready to help out if necessary.

   e. Repeat steps a–d for each command you plan to teach. Before introducing each new command, review the commands you have already taught. Review them in the same order that you taught them.

   f. Finally, review all the commands in random order.

6. *Optional for more advanced learners:*

   Teach the learners to read the commands they have just learned. Use the following steps:

   a. Write each command on a separate card.

   b. Show and read the first command aloud as you model the action.

   c. Show and read the same command aloud as you do the action with the learners.

   d. Show the card without reading or modeling it. Gesture for the learners to carry out the action. (They should not read the card aloud.)

e. Repeat these steps with each card. Before introducing each new card, review the written commands you have already taught. Review them in the same order that you taught them.

f. Finally, mix up the cards and review the commands in random order.

Suggestions

- Go slowly. If you go too fast, learners are likely to become confused and tense and make mistakes. They will learn best if they are relaxed and feel comfortable with the activity.

- Do not try to teach too many commands at one time. Since you will also be reviewing previously taught vocabulary, introduce no more than four to six *new* commands.

- Call learners by name as you give the commands. This helps learners feel comfortable.

- Tell learners that it is OK to watch each other if they are unsure how to respond to a particular command. (There is no such thing as "cheating" in a TPR activity.)

- Provide whatever support the learners need to be successful. TPR activities should not be used to test learners. They are supposed to ensure that learners don't fail. If learners are not successful in carrying out a command, you have either gone too fast, included too much material, or asked them to do something you did not adequately teach and model.

- You can also do a TPR lesson using the steps in a familiar task such as baking a cake or addressing an envelope.

Activity 4

TPR: Body Movements

Purpose

To teach basic action words to very beginning-level learners

How

1. Place three chairs next to each other at the front of the room. Leave enough space in front of the chairs for you and the learners to carry out the following activities.

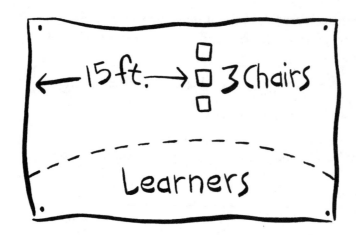

2. Ask two learners to sit in the two outer chairs. You will sit in the middle chair.

3. Teach:

> *Stand up.*
> *Sit down.*

   a. Stand up as you say "Stand up."

   b. Gesture to the learners to stand up.

   c. Sit down as you say "Sit down."

   d. Gesture to the learners to sit down.

   e. Stand up again as you say "Stand up."

   f. Gesture to the learners to stand up again.

   g. Sit down again as you say "Sit down."

   h. Gesture to the learners to sit down again.

   i. Look at each learner in turn and then say "Stand up." You should remain seated as you do this. Use a gesture if necessary. (You are checking the learners' ability to respond to the command without your modeling it for them. If they still do not seem to understand, model the command again by standing up as you gesture to them to stand up.)

4. Then teach:

> *Walk.*
> *Stop.*
> *Turn around.*

   a. Begin walking forward as you say "Walk."

   b. Gesture to the learners to walk with you.

c. As you all walk forward, repeat the word "Walk."

d. Stop walking suddenly and say "Stop."

e. Gesture to the learners to stop.

f. Walk forward again as you say "Walk."
   (If necessary, gesture to the learners to walk also.)

g. After a few steps, stop walking again as you say "Stop."
   (If necessary, gesture to the learners to stop also.)

h. As you turn around to face the three chairs, say "Turn around."

i. Gesture to the learners to turn around.

j. Say "Walk" as you gesture to the learners to walk toward their chairs. Remain standing where you are as they walk forward. (If they do not seem to understand, model walking for them as you repeat the word *Walk*.)

k. After a few steps, say "Stop."

l. Walk forward to catch up with the learners. Stand between them.

m. Say "Walk" without using any gesture. Remain standing where you are as the learners again walk toward the chairs.

n. When the learners reach their chairs, say "Stop."

o. Walk forward and stand between them, facing the chairs.

p. Say "Turn around" as you turn around.
   (The learners should turn around, too. Use gestures if needed.)

q. Say "Sit down."

   (Be ready to model this since the command *sit down* came in the early part of the instruction, and the learners may not remember it very well.)

r. When the learners sit down, make a point of clapping enthusiastically for them as you gesture to the rest of the learners to do the same.

5. You can introduce the vocabulary words *slowly* and *fast* by adding them to the above commands. (Example: *Walk slowly.*) Then teach each new command according to the steps shown above.

Suggestion

If you are teaching a class or small group, do the above activity with two learners. When you finish, you can invite other learners to come to the front of the room and carry out the same commands.

Activity
5

TPR: Foam Balls

Purpose

To introduce speaking using TPR

How

1. Throw a soft foam ball to Learner A, saying, "[Name], catch the ball." When Learner A catches the ball, say, "[Name], throw the ball to me." Use appropriate gestures to convey your meaning.

2. Throw the ball to Learner B, saying, "[Name], catch the ball."

3. Ask, "Who has the ball?" Model the answer: "[Name] has the ball."

4. Call on two or three learners by name and gesture for them to repeat this response. (Model again if necessary.)

5. Tell Learner B, "[Name], throw the ball to [name of Learner C]."

   (If necessary, use gestures to convey your meaning. Point to Learner B and make a throwing gesture in the direction of Learner C.)

6. By making a beckoning gesture with your hand (and mouthing the statement if necessary), encourage Learner B to say to Learner C, "[Name], catch the ball."

7. Call on other learners and ask, "Who has the ball?" Model the appropriate answer as needed.

8. Ask learners to continue to throw the ball to each other while they say, "[Name], catch the ball." Each time the ball is caught, you will ask two or three learners, "Who has the ball?"

9. Provide help as needed, modeling correct responses and encouraging the learners to speak—not just throw and catch.

Vocabulary Drills

You can also use vocabulary drills to teach new vocabulary. Unlike TPR activities, vocabulary drill activities always require learners to give an oral response. These drills can also enable learners to interact with each other as they handle or point to objects or as they talk about the objects using their new vocabulary.

The following are some general principles for doing vocabulary drills:

1. Even if learners can already read English, it is always best if they acquire new vocabulary orally first. After they have heard and practiced new

words orally several times, you can write the new words to show them the written form.

2. Take the time to explain any new words that come up during the activity but that you had not planned to teach.

3. Encourage questions, and don't worry if unexpected conversations take place.

4. When teaching vocabulary or grammatical structures, make sure that the learners always say what is true for them. For example, you might point to one learner's book. Say, "This is *my* book." When the learner repeats the statement, it will be true for the learner. If you said, "This is *your* book," the statement would not be true when the learner repeated it.

6 Vocabulary Drill: Objects

Purpose

To teach a series of new and related vocabulary words

How

(The words taught in the following example happen to be the names of personal hygiene items, but the same steps apply to any category of items. You can teach the names of fruits, vegetables, tools, coins, or any other set of objects using vocabulary drills.)

1. Before the class session, gather two examples of each of the following items: hairbrush, toothbrush, comb, bar of soap.

   (Don't choose two identical items. For example, use a comb with a handle and a comb without a handle; use bars of soap that are different colors.)

2. Choose three volunteer learners to come to the front of the room.

3. Teach: | *hairbrush* |

   a. Pick up a hairbrush and say to the three learners, "This is a hairbrush." Pick up the second hairbrush and say, "This is a hairbrush."

   b. Give one of the hairbrushes to Learner A while saying again, "This is a hairbrush." Beckon to the learner to repeat your words.

   c. Beckon to the learner to repeat again as you say, "This is a hairbrush."

   d. Say to Learner A, "[Name], give the hairbrush to [name of Learner B]." Gesture toward Learner B as you say this.

e. Say to Learner B, "This is a hairbrush." Beckon the learner to repeat.

f. Say to Learner B, "[Name], give the hairbrush to [name of Learner C]." Gesture toward Learner C as you say this.

g. Say to Learner C, "This is a hairbrush." Beckon the learner to repeat.

h. Say to Learner C, "Give the hairbrush to me." Reach for the hairbrush as you speak.

i. Hold the hairbrush so that all the learners can see it. Say, "This is a hairbrush." Then add, "What's this? This is a hairbrush."

4. Review

   a. Give the hairbrush to Learner A and ask, "What's this?"
      (If necessary, help the learner respond, "This is a hairbrush" by beckoning and mouthing the response.)

   b. Give the hairbrush to each of the other learners and ask "What's this?" (Help them give the correct response if necessary.)

5. Teach:

   | *comb* |

   a. Pick up one of the combs and say, "This is a comb." Do the same with the second comb.

   b. Give one of the combs to Learner A and ask, "What's this?" If necessary, beckon the learner to say, "This is a comb."

   c. Say to Learner A, "[Name], give the comb to [name of Learner B]." Gesture toward Learner B as you say this.

   d. Say to Learner B, "This is a comb." Beckon the learner to repeat.

   e. Say to Learner B, "[Name], give the comb to [name of Learner C]." Gesture toward Learner C as you say this.

   f. Say to Learner C, "This is a comb." Beckon the learner to repeat.

   g. Say, "Give the comb to me," gesturing for the learner to do so.

6. Review

   a. Hand the hairbrush to Learner B and ask, "What's this?"

   b. Hand the comb to Learner C and ask, "What's this?"

   c. Ask the learners to give the hairbrush and the comb back to you.

7. Repeat this process for the toothbrush and the soap. Each time you introduce a new object, review the word(s) for the previous object(s) by using the phrase "What's this?" Review the words in the order that you taught them.

Suggestions

- Giving learners the items to hold in their hands helps them relate the new word to the object. (If you are using pictures, hand the picture to the learner.) Reviewing all the previous items after each new one is introduced aids learner retention.

- With more advanced learners, you can expand your questions: "Do you own a hairbrush?" "Do you carry a comb with you?"

- Be alert to learners' tendency to say "a soap." Do not try to explain the difference between count and noncount words (those that generally cannot be preceded by *a* or *an* and whose plural forms require phrases like the following: two *bars of* soap, two *loaves of* bread, two *pairs of* pants, two *cups of* water). Instead, just remodel the correct response and ask them to repeat: "This is soap."

7 Vocabulary Drill to Teach Direction Words

Purpose

To teach the English directional words *left, right, above, below*

How

1. Choose several objects whose names the learners already know. The following example uses tools: a hammer, a screwdriver, a wrench, and a pair of pliers.

2. Ask two or three learners to come to the front of the room. Ask the other learners to observe.

3. Arrange the tools on the table. Review the names of the tools with the learners, using the question *What's this?* Reteach the words if the learners are not sure of them.

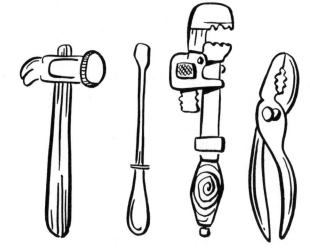

4. Sit down next to (not across from) the first learner. Sitting next to the learner will be important in teaching *left* and *right*. (Sitting across from the learner can cause confusion: "Whose left? Yours or mine?")

5. Place a piece of paper (or a magazine or similar object) on the table.

6. Teach:

> *left*
> *right*

   a. Place the hammer to the left of the piece of paper and say, "The hammer is on the left."

   b. Repeat the statement and beckon for the learner to say it after you.

   c. Move the hammer to the right of the piece of paper. Say, "The hammer is on the right." Beckon for the learner to repeat the statement after you.

   d. Gesture for the learner to be silent. Then say, "Where's the hammer? The hammer is on the right." Repeat both the question and the answer.

   e. Ask the question again ("Where's the hammer?"). Beckon the learner to respond. Help if necessary.

   f. Move the hammer back to the left of the piece of paper and ask the learner, "Where's the hammer?" Beckon the learner to respond.

   g. Repeat step 6 using the screwdriver.

   h. Ask the second learner to take the first learner's chair. Do step 6 with the second learner, using the wrench and the pliers.

7. Teach:

> *above*
> *below*

   a. Hold the hammer above the table and say, "The hammer is above the table."

   b. Ask the learner, "Where's the hammer?" If the learner is unable to respond correctly, model the correct answer again and beckon the learner to repeat it.

   c. Put the hammer below the table and say, "The hammer is below the table." Ask the learner, "Where's the hammer?" Model the answer again if the learner has difficulty responding.

8. As the learners learn more, you can have them place the tools themselves and ask each other where the tools are. The above steps are just the introduction to direction words.

Suggestion

You can use these same steps to introduce other direction words and prepositions such as *next to, on top,* or *in front of.*

Reinforcing Vocabulary

It's important to provide plenty of opportunities for learners to review any new vocabulary. Only through repeated use will they come to "own" it and be able to use it outside the class. Follow-up games, role plays, and simulations of real-world situations all help learners internalize new vocabulary and connect it to their daily lives.

The follow-up activity below is specially designed to reinforce new vocabulary. Activities #14–22 in the "Conversation" section are also appropriate for this purpose.

 Activity 8 Eating Utensils

Purpose

To help learners review vocabulary related to eating utensils, directional words, prepositions, and commands. This activity is particularly useful with beginning-level learners.

How

1. Review the vocabulary the learners will be using: *pick up, put, left, right, on top of, in front of, under, above, cup, bowl, plate, knife, fork,* and so on. (Again, you will have already taught this vocabulary in a previous lesson.)

2. Demonstrate the activity below with one of the learners as the others watch. You will give the instructions. The learner will follow them.

3. After you finish the demonstration, place learners in groups of three. Two of the learners in each group (Learners A and B) should sit next to each other on one side of a table. The third learner (Learner C) should sit across the table facing them. During the activity, each learner will take a turn at these three roles: giver of instructions, receiver of instructions, and observer.

4. Give one set of eating utensils (cup, bowl, plate, knife, and fork) to Learner A and an identical set to Learner B.

5. Give each group a folded cardboard "tent" for use as a table divider.

6. Have Learner B face away from the table. Tell Learner C to arrange the eating utensils (in any configuration) in front of Learner A.

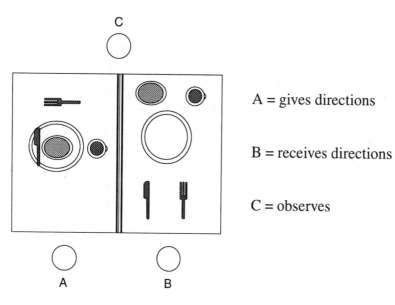

A = gives directions

B = receives directions

C = observes

7. Place the cardboard divider on the table between Learner A and Learner B so that Learner B will not be able to see Learner A's utensils. (Learner A will need to see Learner B's utensils, however, to give Learner B any needed direction during the activity.)

8. When the divider is in place, tell Learner B to turn around to face the table but not to look at Learner A's utensils.

9. Ask Learner A to tell Learner B how to arrange the utensils so that they match Learner A's arrangement. Learner A can use only English and should not use gestures. ("Pick up the cup and put it on top of the plate." "Put the fork to the left of the bowl.") Learner A should watch what Learner B does and make verbal corrections where necessary. ("No, to the *left* of the bowl, not the right. Yes, that's it.")

10. When learners are doing this activity for the first time, don't increase the pressure by setting a time limit. Let everyone try to complete the task. Offer help or encourage the observers to do so if anyone has problems.

11. When Learner A completes the task, have the learners in each group change roles and repeat the task. Then have them change roles again and repeat the task once more. In this way, all three people in each group have an opportunity to play all three roles.

12. The next time the class does this activity, you can set a three-minute time limit to add to the challenge.

Suggestions

- In a one-to-one teaching situation, you and the learner can alternate the roles of giver and receiver of instructions. Since there will be no observer, the person giving the instructions also takes on the observer's tasks.

- You can do the same activity using paper cutouts of geometric shapes (circle, square, etc.) instead of eating utensils. Be sure that the learners already know the names for the shapes.

- Use pictures in place of real objects.

- Have a competition among the groups to see who can complete the task in the shortest amount of time. In this case, Learner C becomes the timekeeper.

Grammar

Grammar is the structure of a language. It is the set of rules specifying the ways words are inflected (how endings are added to change the meaning) and the ways individual words can be combined into larger units to form phrases, clauses, or sentences. Learning individual vocabulary words is helpful, but an ESL learner will be unable to communicate without also understanding English grammatical structures.

During your lessons, you will be trying to replicate actual situations in the outside world in which learners have to use English to get their needs met. When possible, you should try to incorporate the teaching of grammar into these real-life contexts rather than present it in isolation. In this way, learners will be better able to actually use the grammar when they need it. This method of teaching grammar is part of the communicative approach to language instruction.

An example of teaching grammar in isolation might be the following: You are working with a group of learners who already know the word *walk,* and you want to teach the past tense *walked.* You could do the following:

- Say, "I walk to the window" while you do the action.

- Sit down after doing the action and say, "I walked to the window."

- Have the learners repeat each of these sentences.

- Have the learners practice saying pairs of sentences using familiar verbs that have a /t/ sound in the past tense.

    I kick the ball.
    I kicked the ball.

Learners can and do learn this way. But they seem to learn much better when they are involved in activities that give them a chance to use grammar in contexts that are relevant to their real lives. Many ESL texts contain activities that teach grammar in context, so you will not have to create all of these activities yourself. Examples of such "in-context" activities include the following:

- recipes to teach count (egg) and noncount (milk) words

- a game of catch using Total Physical Response (see Activity #5) to teach the following:

Pronouns as direct objects: "Throw the ball to [Name]."
                             "Throw *it* to [Name]."

Pronouns as objects of prepositions:
"Throw the ball to Anna."
"Throw the ball to *her.*"

- pictures of famous people to teach relative clauses:
"He is the president who . . ."

If learners are having difficulty mastering a specific grammatical form, you can stop the activity and spend a few minutes doing a repetitive drill such as the one described below in Activity #9. After completing the drill, return to the original activity and give the learners another chance to use the new grammatical form in context.

Substitution Drills

Purpose

To provide practice using personal pronouns in prepositional phrases

How

(You can use this substitution drill if you have already taught the object pronouns and are now doing an activity [such as the game in Activity #5] that requires the learners to use them. If you find that the learners are having difficulty using the pronouns during the activity, stop and do the substitution drill. Then return to the activity and give the learners another opportunity to use the pronouns.)

1. Say the following sentence and ask a learner to repeat it:
   "Throw the ball to me."

2. Say the pronoun and repeat the sentence:
   "*Me.* Throw the ball to me."

3. Ask the learner to say the sentence again.

4. Say another pronoun and substitute it in the same sentence:
   "*Him.* Throw the ball to him."

5. Ask the learner to repeat the new sentence.

6. Say another pronoun as a cue word: *"Her."*

7. Ask (or gesture for) the learner to say the same sentence, substituting the new pronoun: "Throw the ball to her."

8. Do a random review with the other learners. Say the cue word and have them say the sentence using that word.

10   If Bob Whistles Again, I'll Scream

Purpose

To teach present *real* conditional sentences. (The present *real* conditional refers to a situation in which there is a probability that an event will occur.)

How

1. Write your name and the name of each learner on the chalkboard.

2. Pick one of the names. Ask the learners to identify one habit or behavior that is typical for that person. (You may have to give one or two examples first to get the learners involved.)

3. Do the same with each of the other names.

4. As the learners talk, write their ideas on the board in complete sentences.

   Example: *Bob whistles all the time.*
   José is always late for class.
   Wong wears a tie every day.
   Trang speaks Vietnamese in class.

5. Pick one of the sentences and turn it into a conditional statement. Write it below the original sentence.

   Example: *If Bob whistles again, I'll scream.*

6. Pick another sentence. Beneath it, write the first part of a sentence using the conditional tense.

   Example: *If José is not late tomorrow, I'll . . .*

7. Ask the learners to complete the sentence. Provide help as needed.

   Example: *If José is not late tomorrow, I'll be surprised.*

8. Ask the learners to look at the other sentences on the board and create new ones using the conditional tense. Write these on the chalkboard as the learners say them.

Suggestions

- Allow the learners to have fun with this activity. Encourage them to be creative.

- This activity works best with learners who already know each other well enough to be able to recognize one another's behavior patterns.

(Adapted from Mike Levy, "The First and Second Conditionals" in *Recipes for Tired Teachers,* Christopher Sion, ed. © 1985 by Addison-Wesley Publishing Company, Inc. Reprinted by permission of Longman Publishers.)

Purpose

To teach present *unreal* conditional sentences and to give the learners a break in the lesson as they imagine something they might like to do. (The present *unreal* conditional refers to a situation that is contrary to fact or not the case. The speaker is imagining what would happen if the situation were different from what it actually is.)

How

1. Tell the learners that you want to talk about the state lottery. Bring in a newspaper ad about the lottery to aid the discussion. Read this to the group.

2. Facilitate a discussion about the lottery—how often during the week drawings occur and the amounts of money that can be won.

3. Read or tell a story about someone who actually won a lottery.

4. Tell the learners that you want them to imagine that they have won the lottery: "Can you imagine winning the state lottery? What would you do if you won the lottery?"

5. Have everyone close their eyes for a minute and visualize what it would be like to win the lottery.

6. Share your own thoughts, using the conditional clause, "If I won the lottery, I would . . ." This will help get the ball rolling as well as demonstrate the appropriate language for learners to use.

7. Invite one learner to share his or her thoughts. Tell the person to use the same conditional clause. Provide help if needed.

8. Ask the learners to discuss in pairs or small groups what they would do if they won the lottery.

9. After a few minutes of group discussion, ask for volunteers to share their dreams with the rest of the class.

10. Provide the learners with other examples of the *If/would* expression:

    If Bill asked Helen to marry him, she would say yes.
    If my brother visited us at Christmas, I would be very happy.

Suggestions

- If you live in a state that has no lottery, or if you would prefer not to talk about the lottery with ESL learners, you can adapt this activity by simply asking the learners what they would do if they had a million dollars.

- Use follow-up questions to extend both the discussion and the language practice.

  For example, one learner might say,
  > "If I won the lottery, I would travel around the world."

  You could then ask, "How long would your trip last?"
  > "What kinds of transportation would you use?"
  > "Would you take anyone else with you?"
  > "What countries would you visit?"

  You can involve other learners, too, with questions like
  > "Who else would like to go on this trip?"
  > "What countries would *you* visit, [Name]?"

- If you wish to bring reading and/or writing into this activity, you can write some of the responses on the board as learners say them, or you can ask learners to write their own responses after they've discussed them. If appropriate, you could ask each learner to write a short paragraph that tells about what the learner would do and why.

Activity 12

This Must Be New York

Purpose

To use pictures to teach the modal auxiliaries *must, should, might,* and *could*

How

1. Select several pictures appropriate for reinforcing the use of modal auxiliaries.

2. Show one of the pictures. Then say one of the modals and call on a learner to make a sentence using that particular modal. Give a couple of examples yourself before the person begins. Examples:

Picture	Modal Auxiliary	Sentence
the Statue of Liberty	**must**	This **must** be New York.
a boy coming into the house with muddy shoes	**should**	He **should** wipe his feet first.
a person waiting in line	**might**	She **might** have to wait a long time.
a wrapped gift box	**could**	It **could** be a shirt.

Suggestions

- Look for pictures that show people involved in doing things.

- Ask the learners to look for pictures in magazines that can be used to create sentences using modal auxiliaries.

- Note: *Must* is used here to express probability. The Statue of Liberty indicates that this is probably a picture of New York. This is different from the other meaning of *must* which expresses necessity. Example: Everyone *must* get permission first.

- You can also use pictures to introduce the other modals *(can, would, may, shall)*.

- If learners have difficulty coming up with a sentence, help by asking leading questions. Examples:

  "What city *must* this be?"

  "What *should* the boy do before he comes in the house?"

  "How long *might* the person have to wait in line?"

  "What *could* be in the box?"

Idioms

Learners won't be fully prepared to understand English unless they understand idioms. An idiom is a group of words that means something different from what the individual words might suggest. Idioms can be two- or three-word verbs, such as:

- *call off* (cancel)

- *get across* (convey an idea)

- *think up* (invent)

- *read up on* (get information about)

- *cut down on* (lessen)

Idioms can also be expressions, such as:

- *in the long run*
- *push over the edge*
- *through thick and thin*

The difficulty with idioms is that a learner might already know the meaning of the individual words but not be able to use this knowledge to decipher the idiom's "new meaning."

As a tutor, you need to teach common English idioms that learners need to know and use. But you also need to be aware of your own use of idioms in the classroom. If learners look confused, it may be because you just used an idiom that sounds strange in its literal translation. This is your cue to teach the idiom.

The key to teaching an idiom is to put it into context—that is, to create a story or scenario that uses the idiom so the learner can understand it and be able to use it outside of class. A taped conversation is a useful way to present such a story or scenario. Keep in mind that you can teach more than one idiom at a time.

Activity 13

Writing a Conversation to Teach Idioms

Purpose

To teach the meaning of idioms by using them in the context of a conversation

How

1. Select the idioms you want to teach (examples: *all set, call off, take an exam, change his mind, read up on, push over the edge, in the long run*).

2. Write a conversation between two people that incorporates these idioms. Example:

Maria:	Hey, Fred, are things *all set* for Mike's birthday party?
Fred:	I'm sorry, Maria, but we have to *call off* the party.
Maria:	Oh, no! Why?
Fred:	Mike has to *take a history exam* the next day.
Maria:	You can't get him to *change his mind* and come to the party anyway?

Fred: I tried, but he'll just be too busy *reading up on* his American history.

Maria: I guess I understand. Final exams are enough to *push anyone over the edge.*

Fred: We could change the date. *In the long run,* that might be best. Mike will really be ready for a party after the exam!

3. Read the conversation aloud twice. Or play an audiotape of two people having this conversation. This makes it easier for learners to identify the different speakers.

4. Read the conversation one more time. Stop after each sentence to discuss the meaning of the idiom(s) used in that sentence.

Suggestion

Remember that the conversation serves only as a tool to help you teach the idioms in a meaningful context. Don't teach the conversation as a dialogue or ask the learners to memorize it.

Conversation

ESL learners need to have conversations with English speakers almost every day in a variety of community settings—settings such as the doctor's office, the supermarket, the post office, or their children's school. Tutors need to be aware of the learners' living, work, and family situations to identify the particular settings where learners most need or want to use conversational English. Tutors also need to find out about the learners' future work-related or educational goals to develop conversation activities that will help learners in their daily lives.

The activities described below are specially designed for teaching conversation. They all provide valuable practice, giving learners a chance to hear and feel how everyday language works. They can help give even very beginning learners the confidence that they will be able to participate in basic conversations.

Dialogues and role plays are two of the most useful activities for teaching conversation skills.

Dialogues (see Activity #14) are brief scripts related to everyday tasks such as asking for directions, asking what something costs, or buying stamps at the post office. Dialogues are very good for general practice. They provide learners with "stock phrases" to use in conversations. They also give valuable practice in *initiating* conversations. Being able to ask questions in order to begin a conversation enables learners to be proactive in getting their needs met. They no longer have to sit and wait for someone else to ask a question or start the conversation, as happens in many ESL classrooms.

60

Role plays (see Activity #15) are the natural extension of dialogues. A dialogue is not complete without its corresponding role play. The role play allows learners to go beyond a set script and begin using their own words and ideas. A role play builds on the dialogue just learned. It allows learners to respond in their own words to new thoughts that you or others introduce during the exchange.

The role play adds depth and realism to the dialogue. Now learners must make their own decisions about what to say and how to say it. They become more focused on getting their ideas across than on "saying the lines" as they did for the dialogue. The role play helps learners develop the ability to think on their feet and to ask questions to get information they need. It also reassures them that they will be able to understand native English speakers who won't necessarily use the same words and expressions taught in a classroom dialogue. The dialogue/ role play combination is a cornerstone of the communicative approach, in which classroom activities are related to the real world. See Activities #16 and #21 for other role-play activities that do not build on previously taught dialogues.

14 Dialogues: Basic Steps

Purpose

To give learners initial practice using English in situations similar to those they will encounter in daily life

How

Do the preparation

1. Work with the learners to identify a setting or situation in which they need to be able to use English (for example, a post office).

2. Identify one activity that commonly takes place in that setting (buying stamps). Do not try to focus on every possible interaction that could take place there.

3. Decide who the two people in the dialogue will be (postal clerk and customer).

4. Decide how long the dialogue will be. Three complete exchanges are about right for beginning learners. At this level, dialogues should be simple and brief.

5. Write the dialogue on a piece of paper. (The learners will not see this, but you will need a written version to teach from. For this teaching approach, you teach the dialogue orally. The oral approach keeps the learning experience authentic and immediate.)

Example of post office dialogue:

Postal clerk:	Next!
Customer:	I'd like ten stamps, please.
Postal clerk:	What kind?
Customer:	First-class.
Postal clerk:	That'll be [total cost].
Customer:	Thank you.

6. Decide what props or pictures you will need for teaching the dialogue (for example, pictures of the inside and outside of a post office, first-class stamps, several one-dollar bills, and the change you will need). Props and pictures are especially important in helping beginning learners envision the setting for the dialogue. With more advanced learners, you can establish the setting verbally.

Do the pre-teaching

7. Pre-teach any new vocabulary words the learner will need to know *(next, stamps, first-class)*.

8. Pre-teach any new grammatical structures the learner will need to know *(I'd like . . .)*.

Teach the dialogue to one learner

Key Teaching Steps

1. Tutor recites whole dialogue (both parts) 2–3 times.

2. Tutor takes 1st role; learner takes 2nd role.

3. Tutor and learner reverse roles.

Recite the whole dialogue yourself.

9. Select one learner.

10. Gesture for the learner to listen as you speak.

11. Recite the entire dialogue (both persons' parts) two or three times. As you say each part, move back and forth physically between the two imaginary

positions of the speakers in the dialogue. This visual cue will help the learner differentiate between the two roles. Also use whatever props are necessary to indicate the nature of the conversation between the two speakers.

You take one role and the learner takes the other role.

12. For the first run-through of a new dialogue, you will always take the role of the first speaker so that you can initiate the dialogue.

13. If the dialogue requires props, give the appropriate props to each person (money to the learner/customer, stamps to yourself/clerk).

14. Do the complete dialogue with the learner. Whenever you are about to speak, use the stop gesture to indicate that the learner should listen. When the learner is supposed to speak, use the beckon gesture. If necessary, "mouth" or whisper the lines to encourage the learner to repeat after you.

Reverse roles.

15. Reverse roles (and props, if necessary). Mouth or whisper the first line yourself and then beckon the learner to say it after you.

Involve other learners

16. Call on another learner to do the same dialogue with you. Repeat steps 10–15.

17. Call on two learners to practice the dialogue with each other. Position yourself nearby to help as needed.

Suggestions

- Another example of a dialogue is a common greeting:

Person A:	Hello, how are you?
Person B:	Fine, thanks. How are you?
Person A:	Fine, thanks.

- You can "recycle" dialogues you have already taught by rewriting them to add more detail. For example, in the case of the post office dialogue, the customer could buy special commemorative first-class stamps or mail a package.

- If you find dialogues in ESL texts that seem promising but are too long or complicated, you can rewrite them to a simpler format.

- See p. 38 for descriptions of useful gestures (*listen, stop,* and *beckon*) to use when teaching.

Role Plays

Purposes

To give learners an opportunity to use newly learned words and expressions in conversation without the pressure of having to speak "correctly." To increase learners' confidence in being able to use English to meet their needs in the outside world.

How

1. Teach the learners a basic dialogue related to a specific situation (see Activity #14).

2. When the learners are comfortable with the basic dialogue, ask one learner to come to the front of the room to do a role play with you.

3. Pass out any props needed for the role play.

4. Take the role of the first speaker. Say the same line you practiced in the dialogue. Then beckon the learner to give the next line.

5. Modify your second line of the dialogue slightly to see how the learner will respond. Example from the post office dialogue:

Postal clerk:	Next!
Customer:	I'd like ten stamps, please.
Postal clerk:	First class?
Customer:	Yes.
Postal clerk:	Did you say ten?
Customer:	Yes, please.
Postal clerk:	That's [total price].
Customer:	Thank you.

6. Call another learner to the front of the room to do a role play with you. This time, modify the dialogue even more. Example:

Postal clerk:	Next!
Customer:	I'd like ten stamps, please.
Postal clerk:	What kind of stamps? U.S. or international?
Customer:	U.S.
Postal clerk:	Ten first-class stamps?
Customer:	Yes, please.
Postal clerk:	That'll be [total price].
Customer:	Thank you.

7. If the learners seem comfortable with role plays, have two of them try a role play on their own. Encourage them to be creative. The process may be difficult for them at first, so be ready to encourage and guide the learners as needed.

Suggestions

- You can introduce a new character (yourself or another learner) into the role play to challenge learners to use their conversation skills to meet a changing situation. Example: The customer's neighbor enters the post office. The neighbor greets the customer and asks her where she's going after she leaves the post office.

- Learners might use incorrect English that is quite different from the original dialogue. That's OK if what they say is meaningful and would allow them to get their needs met in the outside world. Example:

Postal clerk:	Next!
Customer:	Me want stamp—ten.
Postal clerk:	What kind of stamps? For the U.S. or international?
Customer:	Mail my country.
Postal clerk:	What country is that?
Customer:	Mexico.

- More advanced learners can do a role play without the preliminary dialogue. You can simply pre-teach any vocabulary words you think are necessary. Role plays can also be generated by activities other than dialogues. For examples, see Activities #16 and #21.

Activity
16

The Language Wheel

Purpose

To help learners develop the oral skills needed for use in specific situations in their everyday lives. (This activity is a good method for helping learners bridge from the ESL session to the outside world.)

How

1. Give each learner a piece of flip chart paper and a marker. Ask each learner to draw a large circle on the paper and write his or her name in the middle of it.

2. Model this by drawing your own circle on the chalkboard or flip chart paper and writing your own name in the middle.

3. Tell the learners that you want them to think of some places where they speak English in their daily lives. Have them write the names of these places around the inside of the circle.

4. Model this yourself in your own circle. See the example below.

5. Circulate around the room, helping the learners as needed (including help with their writing or spelling).

6. After the learners have listed several places where they speak English, tell them to think of the person or people with whom they typically speak in those places. Tell them to draw lines outward from the edge of the circle at the name of each place and to write down who these people are. Model this for them on your own circle. See the example below.

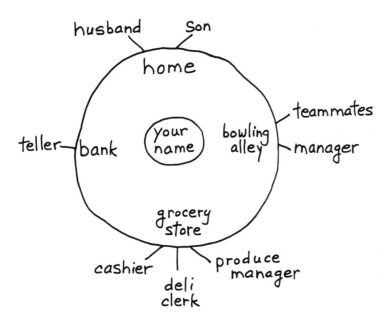

7. Again, circulate around the room, helping learners as needed.

8. After they have completed their work, place learners in pairs. Have the partners take turns briefly describing to each other the people and places on their wheel.

9. Have the first learner in each pair choose one of the places on his or her wheel and explain to the second learner the kind of conversation that might happen with the person or people at that place. Then have the partners switch roles.

10. Have a pair of learners choose one of the places they discussed and do a role play based on a situation that could happen there. Before the role play, have the appropriate learner set the scene by showing the class his or her language wheel and briefly describing the place and the people who will be speaking in the role play.

Suggestions

- If you have not already done role plays with these learners, they may have some difficulty the first time you try this activity. Allow them plenty of time to think of what they want to say, and help them if necessary. (To help learners ease into role plays, you might first want to do a few role plays using pictures. See Activity #21.)

- For a learner who cannot read or write, create a simpler language wheel. Use only two places. Help the learner write the names of the places and people. You can also use a picture or an icon to help the learner remember the words on the wheel—for example, a picture of a stamp for the post office or a book for ESL class.

(Adapted from a presentation given by Anna Cris and Elizabeth Sadler.)

Question Strips

Purpose

To enable learners to initiate conversations on a variety of topics. This activity is especially useful if the learners in your group are at different language skill levels.

How

1. Make up a list of several questions and put them on strips of paper. Write one question per strip. Examples:

   - When was the last time you went to a movie?

   - Have you ever met a famous person? Who?

   - What is your favorite food? Why?

2. Distribute one question strip to each learner.

3. Tell the learners to walk around and find a partner. Have the partners ask each other the questions they have on their strips.

4. After they have answered each other's questions, tell them to trade questions, find new partners, and repeat the process.

5. Continue the activity until learners have partnered with each person in the group or until interest starts to diminish.

Suggestions

- Select topics that the learners are interested in or familiar with. This encourages learners to respond more fully.

- Avoid questions on topics that learners might consider private or inappropriate for discussion because of their cultural background. Similarly, avoid questions that are viewed by Americans as private or inappropriate for public discussion.

- Try to phrase the questions using grammatical structures and vocabulary that are familiar to most of the learners.

- Use questions that are likely to give the questioner *new information.* In natural conversation, people don't ask questions if they already know the answers. For example, questions such as "Where do you live?" or "Do you have any brothers or sisters?" create real communication only if the questioner does *not* already have that information.

- The way you phrase a question can either encourage or limit discussion. With a low-level group, questions that call for one-word or very short answers might be enough. Example: "Do you like ice cream?"

- If you have a multi-level class, the more proficient learners can help the lower-level ESL learners by reading their questions for them.

- To simulate a real-life interaction, encourage the learners to follow up on answers by adding their own comments ("Oh, really? That's my favorite food, too.") or asking questions to get additional information ("What was the name of the movie? How did you like it?"). Such discussion helps learners focus on what's being discussed rather than on how they're saying it.

- With a more advanced group, you can encourage discussion or extended answers by including one or more follow-up questions on the strip. Example: "What was [famous person] like?"

- Question strips can help people learn some of the English conversational conventions that go along with question-and-answer exchanges. Examples:

How to approach a stranger and initiate conversation:
"Excuse me, may I ask you something?"

How to lead up to a question that is culturally acceptable but might seem personal or a bit awkward:
"I hope you don't mind my asking, but . . ."

How to avoid answering a question if the person being asked feels that it's too personal:
"I'm sorry, I'd rather not discuss that."

How to ask for clarification:

"Could you explain that?"

"I'm not exactly sure what you mean."

How to acknowledge what somebody says:

"Really?"

"How interesting!"

18 Who Am I?

Purpose

To give learners an opportunity to practice questions and answers, to use other information they have, and to use critical thinking skills to complete a task

How

1. Write the names of famous people on 3" x 5" cards, one name per card. Prepare one card per learner.

2. Using adhesive tape, stick one card on each learner's back.

3. Have the learners stand up and form pairs. In each pair, the first learner reads the name on the second learner's back. The second learner's task is to find out his or her own "identity" by asking the first learner yes-or-no questions. When the second learner guesses the right answer, the learners switch roles.

4. The learners then form different pairs and repeat the activity.

Suggestions

- Be sure to select names of people that the learners will be likely to know.

- For beginning learners, you can use pictures of famous people instead of writing their names.

- The first time you try this activity, the learners may be somewhat shy or reluctant. Circulate around the room to help and encourage them.

- Use your own judgment about how long to let the activity continue. If the learners seem to be enjoying themselves and are actively involved in discussion, keep things going.

Purpose

To involve learners in a game that encourages them to use their conversation, critical thinking, and persuasive speaking skills

How

1. Tell the learners that they will be playing a game called "Liars."

2. Ask them if they know what the word *liars* means. Explain if necessary.

3. Before beginning the activity, model it for the learners. Tell them four things that you have done in your life. Explain that one of the four things is a lie. Tell the learners to ask you questions to help them identify the lie. Give the learners a few minutes to ask their questions. Then ask them to guess which statement is a lie. If they don't guess correctly, tell them the answer.

4. Tell the learners that each of them will have a chance to be a liar. Give them a few minutes to sit quietly and think of four statements. One must be a lie. Have them write the statements in preparation for the activity.

5. Have the learners form groups of three. Ask each group to pick the first speaker.

6. Give each group three minutes to listen to the speaker's statements and ask questions.

7. Signal them when three minutes are up. Ask each group to guess which statement is the lie.

8. Repeat steps 6–7 for each member of the group.

9. At the end of this part of the activity, ask each group to choose the person that they think did the best job of fooling the other members of the group. Then have these people try to fool the rest of the class. Once again, invite the other learners to ask questions of the "liar." (The members of the person's original group should not participate.)

Suggestions

- When preparing to model your own four statements, choose true statements that might seem hard for the learners to believe and a lie that seems plausible—making your lie more difficult to guess. This will show learners the approach they should take.

- It is best to do this activity after learners have gotten to know each other, rather than during the first few ESL sessions. The fun lies in trying to determine the truth based on what learners already think they know about each other.

- You may choose to vary the time allotted for the activity, but you should give a time limit of some sort so that learners will work quickly.

What's Missing? Jigsaw

Purpose

To generate conversation among learners as they engage in a task that requires them to work together using questioning and answering, negotiating, asking for clarification, and giving directions

How

1. Put learners in groups of three to five.

2. Give each group member a picture. The basic picture is the same, but for each learner a couple of items (different for each learner) will be missing.

3. Tell the learners to look *only* at their own pictures.

4. Tell the learners that their task is to talk among themselves to determine what is missing from their own pictures and then to draw in the missing items. The goal is for all the learners to end up with the same, complete picture.

5. When the learners have completed their task, have one person from each group hold up the completed picture and briefly describe it. (If you want

to do this step, give each of the groups a different picture to work with so that they will not all be describing the same one.)

Suggestions

- Use simple line drawings. Children's coloring books are excellent for this.

- Determine which items can be eliminated in each version. Use correction fluid to blank out those items before photocopying each of the versions.

- For a follow-up activity, you can have the learners write down all the items that they can find in their picture. Or have them write a descriptive paragraph about the picture.

- For beginning learners, a simpler version is to work with a category of items—for example, fruits. Give each learner the same drawing of several fruits, but remove a different fruit from each drawing. The task for each learner is to find out through discussion which fruit is missing (without looking at other pictures). The last step is to draw in the missing fruit in its correct place.

(Adapted from a presentation given by Sue Goldstein.)

21 Teaching with One Picture/Picture Role Play

Purpose

To provide a stimulus for a variety of conversational exercises. Using a single picture, this series of exercises begins with controlled responses and concludes with an open-ended role play.

How

1. Choose a picture or photograph that depicts one or more people.

2. Prepare and write out beforehand all commands and questions for each step in the activity.

3. Display the picture or photograph in full view of the learners. The following steps are based on a photograph represented by the sketch on p. 73.

Physical response only

4. Call on three or four learners in turn. Tell each person to point to various items in the picture. Some sample commands: "Point to a cup." "Point to the woman's hand." "Point to the young man's tie." This is a relatively simple exercise which requires no verbal response from learners. This type of Total Physical Response (TPR) activity is useful with beginning-level learners. (For more information on TPR, see pp. 40–46.)

Yes-or-no answers

5. Call on two or three learners to answer questions that require a yes-or-no answer. For example: "Is the woman standing?" "Are there two men in the picture?" "Is the young man wearing glasses?" This exercise requires the simplest oral response. It can be done with learners at all levels.

Short answers

6. Call on two or three learners to answer questions that require a one-word or short-phrase answer. Examples: "What is in the woman's hand?" "How many people are in the picture?" "Who is wearing the white shirt?" Now you are encouraging the learners to use language of their own to respond to your questions. This is a first step toward active participation in a conversation.

Open-ended questions

7. Call on learners to answer some open-ended questions that build a story. Encourage them to be creative and have fun. Some possible questions and answers:

"How is the woman feeling?"	*("She is not happy.")*
"Why isn't she happy?"	*("She's having a problem with her husband.")*
"Who is the older man?"	*("the woman's father")*
"What is his name?"	*("Frank")*
"What is her name?"	*("Betty")*
"What is her husband's name?"	*("Peter")*

For open-ended questions, prepare only the first question in advance. Formulate each subsequent question as you go, based on how the learner answered the previous one. Your learners are now having a conversation with you!

Role play

8. Use the answers to the open-ended questions to build a role play. Encourage learners to relax and enjoy the role play. Throughout the activity, do not correct the learners' errors. Let them experience their roles and express themselves in the ways that come naturally. The spirit of fun should prevail.

   a. Place a chair for each person in the role play at the front of the room. (The number of chairs needed will vary according to the number of characters generated in step 7.)

   b. Ask for a volunteer to play the part of one of the characters.

   c. Invite that character to take a seat.

   d. Ask the person a few questions that are consistent with answers given during the open-ended questions. Examples: "Are you mad at your husband?" "Why or why not?"

   e. Ask for another volunteer to play the role of a second character.

   f. Invite the new character to take a seat.

   g. Ask this person a question or two to involve him or her in the role play.

   h. Continue with this activity for two or three minutes. Add each new character one at a time.

   i. Encourage the characters to speak to each other in their roles.

   j. After the role play has progressed for awhile and the characters have had a chance to express themselves, stop the activity and thank the learners for their help.

Suggestions

- In a one-to-one situation, lead the learner through the above process. Use a picture with only two characters. You will take one role while the learner takes the other role.

- During the role play, you may find it necessary to do something to keep the exchange going. If so, ask leading questions or make suggestions of your own about the people or events in the picture. For example, you have a picture of two men seated at a lunch counter. You have just set up the role play. You might say, "Sam, you look surprised. Did Michael say something that surprised you?"

- A role play does not always develop as planned. It can be difficult for some learners to speak in a second language about things that are not actually true for them. ESL learners who are not very fluent in English may find it quite difficult to come up with English expressions and make up a story at the same time. If learners have difficulty giving an answer to any of your questions, rephrase the question to require a simpler answer. Example: "Is this man your friend?" instead of "How well do you know this man?" Go slowly and give the learners plenty of time to think and formulate their responses.

- Do not correct errors during the role play. The purpose of a role play is to encourage free use of English under moderately challenging circumstances. Its value lies in allowing learners to communicate freely in English without having to worry about precision.

- You may find that the learners cannot do all the steps in this activity because they do not yet have the necessary English ability. Their ability levels will determine how far they can go. Open-ended questions and role plays may be too advanced for some learners.

(This teaching technique for using a single picture is adapted from *Teacher to Teacher,* © 1988 by City University of New York, published by New Readers Press. Used by permission.)

Activity 22 Meeting and Greeting: Conversation Practice

Purpose

To give learners practice introducing themselves and engaging in conversation with new acquaintances

How

1. Review with the learners some expressions or phrases used when meeting someone for the first time. Examples:

   "Hello, my name is _____."
   (Handshake is appropriate for this and either of the following.)

   "Hello, nice to meet you. My name is _____."

   "Hello, how are you? My name is _____."

2. Review some of the expressions or phrases one would use to close a conversation. Examples:

   "It was nice meeting you."
   (Handshake is appropriate for this and any of the following.)

   "It was nice to meet you. I hope we'll meet again."

   "Oh, look at the time. I have to go. It was nice to meet you."

   "Would you excuse me, please? I enjoyed talking with you about _____."

3. Describe to the class a scenario in which they might have to introduce themselves in a social setting. For example, they are all at a party being sponsored by the ESL program. The party is an opportunity to meet ESL learners and teachers from other classes.

4. Write the following words where the learners can see them:

   Where from?
   How long in United States?
   Your job?
   Anything else?

5. Tell the learners to stand up and walk around as though they were at a party. They should imagine that they do not know anyone else at the party. They are to approach each other and introduce themselves. They should ask questions based on the words on the chalkboard. They can also talk about other things if they choose to do so. Finally, they should end the conversation and move away to find someone else to meet and talk with.

Suggestions

- Decide how much pre-teaching or practicing of the opening and closing expressions is needed. With beginning learners, do role plays beforehand to give them the opportunity to practice the expressions.

- Once the activity starts, let the learners engage freely in conversation and not worry about how correct they are in their use of these expressions. The same pertains to the questions they will ask each other. By using the simple phrases on the board (instead of complete questions) as stimuli, the learners avoid the tendency to memorize the exact wording of the questions to be asked.

- In a one-to-one situation, the tutor and learner would practice using the various opening and closing expressions with each other. The tutor could set up different scenarios that would require the learner to ask different questions.

The Sounds of English

Learners who have an extensive English vocabulary and a good grasp of English grammar might still be unable to speak the language so that others can understand them. To be understood, a speaker needs to pronounce individual English sounds (phonemes) correctly. But, even more important, the speaker needs to use appropriate English patterns of stress, rhythm, and intonation.

Although this section includes information to help you teach individual English sounds, most of the activities focus on teaching the *patterns* of English speech. There is an important reason for this. American speakers of English will usually be able to understand an ESL learner's speech if the stress, rhythm, and intonation patterns are correct—even though individual sounds are mispronounced. If learners can use correct English speech patterns automatically, they can concentrate on what they want to say, the vocabulary to use, and the proper grammar. They will not have to worry too much about correct pronunciation of individual sounds while they are trying to carry on a conversation. Conversely, even when learners do pronounce the individual sounds correctly, their English can sound foreign—or even be unintelligible—if they use incorrect (non-English) stress, rhythm, or intonation patterns.

The following are helpful guidelines for teaching both sounds and patterns.

When doing activities not specifically related to sounds or patterns

Do not stop to make a correction unless you do not understand what the learner is saying—learners are generally trying hard to focus on meaning during the ESL lesson. Instead, make notes about difficulties the learner is having with individual sounds or with patterns. Pay special attention to problems with patterns. Then set aside separate times for working on these items. Do not mix this practice into other activities.

When doing activities specifically designed for working on sounds or patterns

- Keep sessions short. This type of practice can become tedious.
- Use lots of repetition. Recycle sounds and patterns from one session to the next.

- Use familiar vocabulary. You should not introduce new English vocabulary or structures during this part of the lesson.

- Teach everyday pronunciation and patterns as well as the "textbook pronunciation" and patterns. This helps learners become familiar with the English they will actually hear in the outside world. Examples: "I gotta go now." "Hower you today?"

- Teach pronunciation and patterns in a meaningful context rather than in isolation. Example: If a Spanish speaker is having difficulty making the /i/ sound, as in *bit,* practice a dialogue that includes words with this sound.

  "Excuse me, which aisle are the potato chips in?"
  "Potato chips are in aisle six."

Teaching Individual Sounds

Sounds are not the same as letters. Some letters have more than one sound: for example, *c,* as in *city* and *cup.* Some sounds can be represented in English by different letters or letter combinations: for example, *fix, phone, cough.* The section that follows focuses on the *sounds* of the language, not the letters used to represent those sounds.

This book uses italics to indicate the name of a letter: *b.* It uses slashes to indicate the sound of a letter: /b/. A macron over a letter indicates a long vowel sound: /ā/. A single vowel has a short sound if there is no macron: /a/. Capital letters show a word or part of a word that is stressed: WORKshop.

There are three major reasons why learners have problems with individual sounds.

1. The sound is new to the learner.

   For example, a French speaker learning English is apt to have difficulty with a word like *thank* because French has no /th/ sound. A French speaker tends to say *sank* or *tank* instead.

2. The sound exists in the learner's native language, but comes in a place that is new to the learner.

   For example, an English speaker learning Vietnamese is apt to have difficulty with words like *Nganh* and *Nguyen.* Although English has the /ng/ sound, it does not have the sound at the beginning of words. A Cambodian learning English will tend to drop final /s/ sounds because the Khmer language does not have an /s/ sound at the end of words. The English words *bus* and *peace* might become *buh* and *pea.*

3. The sound doesn't exist in the learner's native language but is similar to one that does.

   For example, a Spanish speaker learning English is apt to have difficulty distinguishing the difference between the vowel sound in the word *bit* and the vowel sound in the word *beat*. The Spanish sound system has the /ē/ sound but not the /i/ sound, so Spanish speakers tend to say both these words with the /ē/ sound.

You can teach sounds in three ways. You can model the sound yourself, have the learners watch your mouth as you make the sound, or describe what is happening in your mouth as you make the sound. Listed below are some examples of terms for describing both what is happening in the mouth and the key features of individual sounds. Appendix B contains a list of English speech sounds and their descriptions.

Continuant/stop

If you can continue the sound as long as you want, it's a continuant. If the sound just stops, it's a stop. Some of the consonant sounds, such as /s/, /m/, and /l/, are continuants, as are all the vowel sounds. The consonant sounds /b/, /p/, and /t/ are examples of stops.

Voiced/unvoiced

If you use your vocal cords when you make the sound, it's voiced. All the vowel sounds are voiced. If you don't use your vocal cords, the sound is unvoiced. Some consonant sounds, such as /z/, are voiced. Others, such as /s/, are unvoiced.

Nasal

If the sound comes from your nose, it's a nasal sound. The sounds /m/, /n/, and /ng/ are nasal sounds.

Front/back

Vowels can be described by the place in the mouth where the tongue "humps" up. An example of a "front vowel" sound is /ē/, as in *feel*. For this sound, the hump is at the front of the mouth. An example of a "back vowel" sound is /oo/ as in *tool*. For this sound, the hump is at the back of the mouth.

Tense/lax

Vowels can be described by the degree of tenseness or laxness of the muscles of the mouth. For example, the /ē/ sound in the word *cheap* makes the mouth feel more tense than the /i/ sound in the word *chip,* although the position of the mouth is almost the same for each of these sounds. Thus, the sounds /ē/ (tense) and /i/ (lax) form a tense/lax pair.

Rounded/unrounded

Vowels can also be described by the rounding or unrounding of the lips during production of the sound. All front vowels are made with lips unrounded (examples: /ē/, /i/, /a/). All back vowels are made with rounded lips (examples: /oo/, /ō/).

Vowel length

Vowel sounds have different lengths, or durations, depending on whether a voiced or an unvoiced consonant follows the vowel, or whether the vowel falls at the end of the word. The vowel sound is shortest in duration when an unvoiced consonant follows the vowel *(seat)*. It is longer when a voiced consonant follows the vowel *(seed)*. It is longest when the vowel sound is at the end of the word *(see)*.

Getting Your Mouth Ready

Purpose

To help learners get their mouths ready as they begin a pronunciation exercise. This activity is also a good activity to use at the beginning of the lesson to help learners improve their general pronunciation.

How

Stretch and breathe

1. Tell the learners to look at your face and do the same thing that you do as you give them instructions. Tell them that these exercises will help them with their English pronunciation.

2. Tell them to make their mouths as large as possible. Demonstrate this.

3. Tell them to close their mouths and puff out their cheeks. Tell them to alternate making their mouths as large as possible and then closing their mouths and puffing out their cheeks. Demonstrate and then do this with them.

4. Tell them to make their faces as wide as possible. This may seem like a strange request, but your demonstration will help.

5. Tell them to make a silent yawn. Demonstrate, exaggerating as you slowly *yaawwnn.*

6. Now tell them to make a noisy yawn. Demonstrate.

7. Repeat the silent yawn and then the noisy yawn.

8. Tell the learners to gently breathe in through their noses, hold their breaths for just a second or two, and then let the air out slowly. Demonstrate this.

9. Tell them to breathe in through their mouths, hold their breath for a second or two, and then let the air out slowly. Demonstrate this.

10. Continue to alternate back and forth a few times between the nasal and oral breathing as the learners follow along with you.

Alternating stress

1. Ask the learners to rest for just a few seconds and relax. Tell them you want them to now repeat some numbers and letters after you. They should listen closely to the way you say the numbers and letters and repeat them exactly.

2. Count from one to four with the stress on the number one. Have the learners repeat after you. Be sure they are all properly stressing the number one.

3. Continue counting from one to four, stressing the next number each time. Have the learners repeat each sequence after you. The following illustrates the pattern:

ONE	two	three	four
one	**TWO**	three	four
one	two	**THREE**	four
one	two	three	**FOUR**

4. Do the same with the letters *a, b, c,* and *d.*

Suggestion

Be sure the learners know the meaning of words that will be used in these exercises. You can also choose to use this occasion to introduce some new words. For example, this may be a perfect opportunity to teach the word *yawn.*

(Adapted from a presentation given by Pat Mathews.)

Minimal Pairs

Purpose

To help learners first hear the difference between two sounds (listening) and then correctly produce each of the sounds (speaking). (A minimal pair consists of two words that differ only in one sound. Examples: *hat/bat, rake/rate, hit/heat.*)

How

1. Identify the two sounds you want to work on. For example, /l/ and /r/.

2. Create a list of words that contrast these two sounds. Examples:

/l/	/r/
lip	rip
lock	rock
lap	rap
late	rate

3. Ask the learner to listen to the difference between the two sounds as you say first the /l/ sound and then the /r/ sound.

4. Ask the learner to listen to the difference again. This time, as you pronounce the /l/ sound, raise one finger. As you pronounce the /r/ sound, raise two fingers.

5. Ask the learner to listen as you say a word beginning with /l/. Raise one finger. Say a word beginning with /r/. Raise two fingers.

6. Read the first pair of words on the list *(lip/rip)*. After you read each word, ask the learner to raise one or two fingers to indicate which sound the word begins with. If the learner has difficulty, demonstrate by saying each word again and raising the appropriate number of fingers.

7. Repeat the process with the first few pairs on the list.

8. When the learner understands what to do, begin alternating between reading the /l/ word first or the /r/ word first.

9. Go back through the list and have the learner repeat the words in pairs after you.

10. Finally, put the words into a meaningful context so the learner has an opportunity to practice saying the two sounds in sentences.

- Say the two words in a pair: "lock/rock."

- Ask the learner to repeat these two words after you.

- Say each word in a sentence. Have the learner repeat the sentence. ("He put the key into the lock." "A large rock fell onto the highway.")

Suggestions

- Instead of raising one finger, you may want to put the numbers *1* and *2* on separate 3" x 5" cards. Have the learner point to or raise the number that corresponds to the sound.

- If possible, use pictures for the final step when introducing the sentences.

Teaching English Patterns: Stress, Rhythm, and Intonation

Stress, rhythm, and intonation are important in defining the patterns that help convey meaning in English.

Stress is the emphasis given to individual syllables within a single word (accent) or phrase. Stressed syllables tend to sound louder to the listener. Examples: *WORKshop, to the MOUNtains.*

Rhythm is the pattern of stresses that occurs when words are put together into sentences. Example: *We GAVE her a PRESent. She LOVED it. The PRESent was a TRIP to the MOUNtains.*

Intonation is the use of pitch (the rise and fall of the voice like notes on a musical scale) to convey meaning; this can be

- to differentiate grammatical forms, e.g., questions

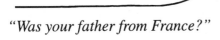

"Was your father from France?"

- to highlight certain words or information

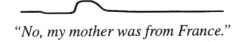

"No, my mother was from France."

Activity 25 — Rubber Bands and Stress/Rhythm Patterns

Purpose

To help learners improve the overall intelligibility of their speech by learning to use correct English stress/rhythm patterns

How

1. Give one rubber band to each learner and take one for yourself.

2. Select the target word, phrase, or sentence that you want the learner to work on. Examples might include

   - something a learner has just said using incorrect stress or rhythm

   - a word that is difficult because it looks similar to a word in the learner's native language but has a different stress pattern (*con-fi-DEN-tial* in English versus *con-fi-den-ci-AL* in Spanish)

   - a part of a dialogue that you plan to teach

   - two words that are similar in sound but have vowel sounds that are held for different lengths of time *(beet, bead)*

3. Use your thumb and forefinger of each hand to hold the ends of the rubber band. Say the target item as you stretch and relax your rubber band to show stress and rhythm or the amount of time a sound is held. Pull the ends farther apart to show words or syllables that are stressed or vowel sounds that are held for a longer time (indicated by capital letters).

   Example 1: length of vowel sound

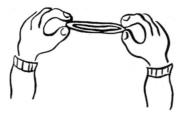

beet (vowel sound followed by a consonant that is unvoiced)

bEAd (vowel sound followed by a consonant that is voiced)

Example 2:   stress or accent within a word

produce: to make

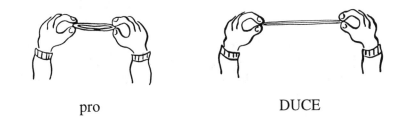

pro   DUCE

produce: fresh fruits and vegetables

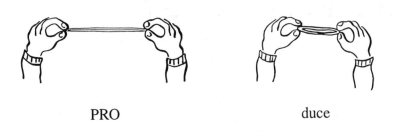

PRO   duce

Example 3:   stress or rhythm pattern in a sentence

Note that in English we usually stress the content words (such as nouns and main verbs) rather than the structure words (articles such as *a* or *an;* prepositions such as *to* and *from;* auxiliary verbs such as *is, will,* or *would;* pronouns such as *you* and *your*). In this example, pull the ends of the rubber band apart for the capitalized words or syllables, and relax the band if the word or syllable is not capitalized.

I would LIKE to go HOME to see my FAMily next summer.

4.   As you stretch and relax the rubber band, you might also want to lengthen the stressed vowel sounds for extra emphasis to help the learner better hear them. Example:

I'm gO-O-O-Oing to the stO-O-O-Ore this afternOO-OO-OO-OOn.

5.   Have the learners repeat the target item(s) as they stretch and relax their own rubber bands.

6.   If the learners have difficulty, say the target item again as you model with your rubber band. Then have the learners repeat the item using their own rubber bands.

Suggestion

An excellent way to help learners practice using English stress and intonation patterns is by having them use rubber bands to practice saying or reading limericks.

(The technique of using a rubber band to teach stress and rhythm was adapted from Judy B. Gilbert, *Clear Speech: Pronunciation and Listening Comprehension in North American English,* Teacher's Resource Book, 2nd ed. © by Cambridge University Press, 1984, 1993. Reprinted with the permission of Cambridge University Press.)

Activity 26 Kazoos and Pitch/Intonation Patterns

Purpose

To help learners improve the overall intelligibility of their speech by learning to use correct English pitch/intonation patterns

How

1. Give a kazoo to each learner and take one for yourself.

2. Select the target sentence or phrase that you want the learners to work on.

3. Say the target item.

4. "Play" the target item on your kazoo, using the normal English pitch and intonation. (In the following examples, the line rises to indicate a rise in pitch.)

   Example 1:   statement

   The dog ate my homework.

   Example 2:   questions that require a yes-or-no answer

   He ate your homework?   *Are you sure?*

Example 3: questions that require an answer other than yes or no

How do you know?

5. Have the learners "play" the item on their own kazoos. There are two advantages of having the learners "play" the item before they try to say it:

   • It helps them temporarily forget about using correct pronunciation and concentrate instead on using correct pitch/intonation.

   • It helps them hear the differences between English pitch/intonation patterns and those of their native language.

6. Have the learners say the item, using the same pitch and intonation patterns they just "played" on their kazoos. This is an important step in reinforcing the learning.

(The technique of using kazoos to teach pitch and intonation was adapted from Judy B. Gilbert, *Clear Speech: Pronunciation and Listening Comprehension in North American English,* Teacher's Resource Book, 2nd ed. (Cambridge & New York: Cambridge University Press, 1993) © by Cambridge University Press, 1984. Reprinted with the permission of Cambridge University Press.)

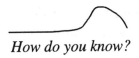

Using Pitch and Stress to Change the Meaning

Purpose

To help ESL learners understand that variations in pitch and stress can result in a change of meaning

How

1. Give a kazoo to each learner and take one for yourself.

2. Write the following statement on a piece of paper. Read it aloud.

   "I lost my hat."

3. Explain that English speakers can change the pitch and stress to emphasize different words in order to modify the meaning.

4. Illustrate this by reading aloud the question below. Then read the answer. The capital letters in bold type indicate where you should use a higher pitch for emphasis.

> "**WHO** lost their hat?"
> "**I** lost my hat."

5. Read the answer aloud again. Then "play" it on your kazoo, using the same pitch pattern.

6. Repeat steps 4 and 5 for the following question/answer pairs:

> "Where **IS** your hat?"
> "I **LOST** my hat."

> "**WHAT** did you lose?"
> "I lost my **HAT.**"

7. Then illustrate the use of pitch in a complete conversation such as the one below. Read the following conversation aloud. (Advanced learners can follow along on their own copies.) The capital letters in bold type indicate where you should use a higher pitch.

> A: What's the **MAT**ter?
> B: I lost my **HAT.**

> A: What **KIND** of hat?
> B: It was a **RAIN** hat.

> A: What **COLOR** rain hat?
> B: It was **WHITE.** White with **STRIPES.**

> A: I found a **RED** one.
> B: No, **MINE** was **WHITE.**

8. Repeat the entire conversation, this time "playing" it on your kazoo.

9. Read the first line of the conversation aloud again. Then "play" the line on your kazoo. Ask the learners to "play" the same line on their kazoos. When they have finished, ask them to say the line aloud.

10. Do the same for each line of the conversation.

Suggestion

Kazoos can also help learners understand how pauses can affect meaning. In the following examples, # indicates a pause:

> Simon asked Lucia, # "Will you marry me?"

> "Simon," # asked Lucia, # "will you marry me?"

(The rain hat story was adapted from Judy B. Gilbert, *Clear Speech: Pronunciation and Listening Comprehension in American English*, Teacher's Manual and Answer Key, © by Cambridge University Press, 1984. Reprinted with the permission of Cambridge University Press.)

Teaching Adults: An ESL Resource Book

Reading and Writing

One definition of "reading" is *a process for deriving meaning from text.* To be successful in this process, a reader must

- utilize effective eye movement
- have a large enough listening and speaking vocabulary to be able to match the printed word to the spoken word
- understand the basic structure (grammar) of the language
- have some prior experience or knowledge about the topic
- have strategies for interacting with the text such as predicting/confirming and identifying cause and effect
- know the "code": the sound(s) of English letters and letter combinations

One definition of "writing" is *the ability to make the written symbols that form the alphabet.* But, writing is also *a process for communicating meaning through print.*

Principles of Teaching Reading and Writing

The following are some general principles to keep in mind when teaching reading and writing to ESL learners.

Treat adult learners as adults.

Adult ESL learners may not be able to speak English very well, and some may be unable to read in any language. But remember that they bring with them a lifetime of other knowledge and experience acquired from their families, friends, communities, jobs, religious institutions, schooling, travels, and more. As an ESL tutor or teacher, you might find yourself working with a farmer who has years of experience growing rice, a seamstress who supports a family of five with her sewing skills, a fisherman with extensive knowledge of marine life, or a midwife who was the sole health care provider in a small rural village.

You can build on the learners' rich backgrounds by respecting their experiences and encouraging them to share these experiences in class. Always be on the lookout for teaching materials that relate to the learners' life skills as well as their language skills. In this way, you will be validating and affirming them as fellow adults.

Teach new words orally first . . .

People should learn the meaning of words by using them orally before trying to read them. This is especially important with beginning-level learners. Decoding new words in print will not be possible unless the learner has first comprehended the meaning orally.

. . . but introduce reading and writing as soon as possible.

Educators don't necessarily agree on when to introduce reading and writing. Those who favor exposing nonliterate adults to print from the beginning give the following reasons:

- Most learners equate education with reading and writing. Reading and writing activities can be highly motivating for learners.

- To function effectively in their everyday lives, learners need to be able to recognize important print words such as *in, out, push, pull, men,* and *women.* They also need to be able to write their names and addresses.

- Reading and writing reinforce the language skills developed through listening and speaking.

- People's learning styles are different. Some people learn better or retain information better by seeing and doing (reading and writing) than by listening and speaking alone.

- Reading and writing are effective tools that learners can use to acquire the information they need.

Establish a context for reading.

ESL learners will encounter many words in print that are unfamiliar to them. Being able to sound out or decode a word will not help if the learner does not know what the word means. Often the learner will be able to read enough words to figure out the general meaning of the passage. But sometimes not knowing a word will make it almost impossible to get meaning from that particular text.

It is much more likely that learners will be able to figure out what the meaning of a word is if they understand the context of the passage. They will also be better prepared to understand the author's message and relate it to their own ideas and experiences. There are several things that you can do to help create context for the learners:

- Use pictures to help bridge the gap between the information in the text and the learners' own knowledge and experience. For example, some learners might not recognize the word *spider*. Such learners would be thoroughly confused in trying to read an article about spiders. An accompanying picture of spiders can provide the needed context, enable the learners to access their store of background knowledge about spiders, and help them narrow down the possibilities when they come to unfamiliar words.

- Use some of the pre-reading activities described in Activity #31 to help provide context and allow the learners to share what they already know about the topic.

- Use the Language Experience Approach (LEA) described in Activities #28–30. In LEA, the learner talks about an experience or an idea, and you write down the learner's exact words. What you have written becomes the reading text. In this case, you don't have to worry about creating context for the learner. The context is already there!

Start with printing.

You may find yourself working with learners who cannot read or write in their own language or whose native language uses a writing system different from that of English (such as Chinese, Thai, Arabic, or Hindi). Such learners will first need to learn to write the letters in the English alphabet. In most cases, the best place to start is with printing (manuscript writing) rather than with cursive writing. Reasons for this include

- It is most similar to the print that learners will see in books, magazines, and newspapers.

- Most forms that learners will need to fill out in daily life require the use of printing.

Activity #43 focuses on learning to print.

Use writing to reinforce reading.

As people learn to read new words, idioms, everyday expressions, and stock phrases, they should also have an opportunity to write them. Writing reinforces the meaning of new words and expressions.

Focus on content, not correctness.

People learn to speak by speaking, to read by reading, and to write by writing. "Mistakes" will be a natural part of that learning process. When people are learning to write, help them focus on the *message they are trying to communicate* rather than on perfectly formed letters, correct spelling, and perfect grammar.

help learners who may be nervous about their writing ability is to
them to write the way they speak. This advice is equally useful for
g-level ESL learners who can already read and write in their native
e and for those who have never written in any language. As learners
become more comfortable with both English and writing, you can focus more
attention on "correctness."

Activities #44–53 give suggestions for helping learners develop their writing
as a tool for communicating meaning.

Language Experience

The Language Experience Approach (LEA) is a simple but powerful technique
for teaching reading to all levels of learners—beginning or advanced. It can be
used with classes, with small groups, or in one-to-one tutoring. In an LEA
activity, the learner tells a story as you write it down. The learner's story provides the content for the reading lesson.

LEA builds on the learner's life experience and treats the learner as a person
with ideas, feelings, and stories that are worth communicating. It is especially
effective because it encourages the learner to use all four basic language skills:
listening, speaking, reading, and writing.

LEA gives learners a welcome opportunity to share what they know and to
read something that they themselves have created. Other advantages of using
LEA include the following:

- Learners are more interested in learning to read if they can read their own
  words on topics of their own choosing.

- Learners feel empowered because you show respect for both them and
  their stories by writing the stories down.

- Learners see the powerful connection between the spoken and written
  word. Although many people take this connection for granted, beginning
  readers may be discovering for the first time that print words are really
  representations of spoken words.

It is important to write the story exactly as the learner tells it. You might think
that not correcting the learner's grammar could reinforce poor English, but
there are several very good reasons for transcribing exactly what the learner says:

- LEA works because it uses the beginning reader's *own* language—not
  someone else's.

- It is easier and more enjoyable for learners to read what they themselves
  have just said. It is more difficult for them to read someone else's words.

- By writing exactly what the learners say, you will be creating a permanent record of progress as well as a rich source of information for planning future lessons.

- The focus of the lesson should be reading, not grammar. Sometimes learners need to have a chance to concentrate on getting meaning from print without being concerned about "correctness."

Activity 28 Creating a Language Experience Story

Purpose

To use materials created from the learner's own words and life experiences as the basis for reading instruction

How

1. Ask the learner to tell you a brief story or share an experience with you.

2. Listen as the learner talks. Stop to ask for clarification if necessary.

3. Tell the learner that you would like to write the story. Ask the person to retell all or part of it.

4. Write *exactly* what the learner says on a piece of paper or flip chart page. Use correct spelling and punctuation, but do not make any grammatical or stylistic changes.

5. Leave a blank line between each line of writing in case you have to add sentences or make changes later.

6. Read the story aloud to the learner, pointing to each word as you read it. (In this way, you are reinforcing the connection between spoken and printed words.)

7. Read the story again in a more natural rhythm.

8. Ask if there is anything the learner would like to add or change.

9. If the learner has some awareness of the English sound/symbol relationship, ask the learner to read each sentence after you read it. Help the learner with any difficult words.

10. Ask which words the learner would like to work on.

11. Circle these words and explain that you will work some more on this story at the next lesson.

12. Review the story at the next lesson. If possible, type the story and make two copies—one for you and one for the learner.

Suggestions

- Use LEA stories to work on the learner's reading skills. Some things you can do:

  - Work on sequencing. Write all the words from one sentence on cards, one word to a card. Mix up the cards and ask the learner to assemble them into a correct sentence. Or write each sentence on a separate card and ask the learner to put the cards in the correct sequence.

  - Do a CLOZE exercise. (See Activity #37.)

  - See Activities #32–34 for some additional ideas for building skills with LEA stories.

- If you are working with a group of learners, find a topic that they all know something about. (See Activity #29 for ideas.) Have the learners take turns adding sentences to the story. Read the completed story to them. Then read the story aloud as a group. Finally, encourage individuals to try reading the story aloud by themselves.

- It is usually best to write the story exactly as the learner tells it. But if you are working with a group, a situation might come up in which one of the learners points out a grammatical error in the story. If this happens, you should make the correction because other learners in the group may become confused if you don't. But first give the learner who provided the sentence an opportunity to tell you how the sentence could be corrected.

- Take your time during this activity. It is important to give learners lots of time to think so that they can say what they really want to say. Learn to wait silently and patiently.

94   *Teaching Adults: An ESL Resource Book*

- Since some learners may be hesitant about relating a personal experience or creating a story, be prepared with questions to generate the initial conversation. Examples:

    What is your favorite hobby? Describe it.

    If you could have three wishes, what would they be?

    What type of work do you do? What do you like and dislike about your work?

    What is the strangest thing that ever happened to you?

    Tell me a story about someone in your family.

- You can also work with the learner to create a semantic web of ideas about a particular topic. (See Activity #48.) The learner can then choose one idea to use as the basis for an LEA story. Often the ideas generated in one web can serve as the basis for several different stories.

- When working with very beginning readers, keep the story short—only two or three sentences. Read the story aloud together before the learner tries to read it alone.

- With beginning readers, you can also use sentence starters as the basis of an LEA activity. Have the learner dictate the rest of the sentence as you write it.

    Examples:

    I want _____.

    I can _____.

    My children are _____.

    I wish _____.

29 Group LEA: Generating a Common Experience

Purpose

To create shared knowledge or experience among a group of learners in preparation for developing a group LEA story

Suggestions

- If all the learners in a small-group or class situation are familiar with the chosen topic or have experienced the same event, they can work collaboratively to create the LEA story. Each learner contributes a sentence or two. For example, you could ask the learners to describe the weather in the local area or describe something that happened recently in the ESL class.

- You can also create a common experience for the learners to have and then work with them to develop an LEA story about it. Some ideas for creating common experiences include

    - Take the learners on a field trip.

    - Ask one of the learners to demonstrate something he or she does well.

    - Show a movie to the group.

    - Read a short story or newspaper article to the group.

    - Take the learners on a walk around the school or neighborhood. Observe trees, plants, buildings, people, or cars.

    - Have learners bring in photographs of their families, friends, or neighborhoods. Discuss the various people and items pictured. Have learners compare and contrast their photographs.

(Many of the above ideas come from Carol N. Dixon and Denise Nessel, *Language Experience Approach to Reading [and Writing]*, © 1983 by Prentice Hall. Used with permission.)

Activity 30 Building Skills with LEA Stories

You can use LEA stories to teach many different skills. Learners are more likely to learn a skill when it is connected to their own words. Work with the learners to choose what skill to work on. This encourages them to take responsibility for directing their own learning. The learners can, for example:

- copy the story in their notebooks for writing practice

- circle every *e* (or some other letter) in the story

- underline every capital letter

- count the number of sentences

- make flash cards for words they would like to learn. Ask the learners to practice with the cards—alone or in pairs—until they can read the words by sight. (See Activity #32.)

- reconstruct one of the sentences from the story with cards (You will need to prepare the cards by writing each word of the sentence on a separate card.)

- make as many words as possible by changing the initial consonant sound in one of the words in the story (see Activity #35), e.g., *went, bent, dent, lent*

- if there are direct quotes in the story, practice reading them with excitement, anger, sadness, boredom, or other emotions

- say words that begin with the same consonant blend as a word in the story, e.g., *start, stop, stuck* (You can write them down as the learners say them and then ask the learners to read them.)

- select a word ending that they have already studied (such as -*s*, -*ing*), practice adding it to different words from the story, and then use each new word in a sentence (The learners can do a similar exercise by deleting endings from words in the story.)

- select a word with a long vowel sound and say what the word would be if the sound were changed to a short vowel, e.g., *made/mad* (You could also reverse the process, e.g., *not/note.*)

- write contractions from the story and say what words they stand for, e.g., *wasn't/was not*

- circle all the adjectives

- give a word or phrase that means the opposite of words you underlined in the story, e.g., *tall/short; got married/got divorced*

- locate on a map the places mentioned in the story

- develop a list of words to learn to spell

- identify cause-and-effect relationships ("Why did this happen?")

- reread the story for fluency

Pre-Reading Activities

Pre-reading activities help provide context for the reading and enable the learners to connect their background knowledge to the reading. Pre-reading activities

- allow learners to approach reading with a better understanding of what they are about to read

- help learners feel prepared

- enable learners to make valid predictions about the content of the reading

- increase the probability that learners will be able to figure out an unfamilar word

  For example, if the learners know that the reading selection is about automobile safety, they can predict what the words in this sentence might be:

  You should wear a _____ _____ when you drive.

- ensure that all the learners in a learning group have access to the same basic background knowledge

Activity 31 Pre-Reading Activity: Discussion

Purpose

To use discussion to develop the learners' base of knowledge about a specific topic before reading something related to that topic

How

1. Tell the learners the topic that they will be reading about.

2. Write the topic on the board. Example: "What to do when you're sick."

3. Involve the learners in a discussion by asking questions that encourage learners to discuss the topic. For this topic, possible questions might be

   What do you do when you get sick?
   Why do you go to the doctor?
   What happens when you go to the doctor?
   What is a prescription?
   What is another way to get medication?

Teaching Adults: An ESL Resource Book

4. *Optional:*

Ask the learners to help you create a list of items that are related to the reading topic, such as "Illnesses" or "Medicines." Help them with the English words if they are having difficulty. (They probably know the names of many medicines in their native language.)

Suggestions

Other ideas for pre-reading activities:

- Use a sentence completion activity to generate discussion. For a reading selection about elections or government, you could ask the learners to complete the following sentence: "If I were president, I would . . ."

- Have the learners help you construct a semantic web showing what they already know about the topic. (See Activity #48.)

- Read the title of the selection aloud and ask the learners to predict what they think it will be about.

- Create an information grid related to the topic, and ask the learners to help you complete it. (See Activity #54.)

- Set a purpose for the reading by asking the learners to find the answer to a specific question as they read.

- Select a picture (or more than one picture, if necessary) related to the topic of the reading. Show the picture to the learners and call on several learners to describe what they see happening in the picture or to imagine what the people in the picture are thinking. You can continue to ask questions about the picture to encourage additional discussion.

Recognizing Words

To obtain meaning from text, a reader must be able to understand the author's message and react to it using prior information and experience. This can't happen, however, if the reader is unable to recognize many of the words in the text.

Recognition is the ability to match words in print with words the reader already uses and whose meaning the reader already knows. Good readers are able to draw on one of five word recognition strategies to do this (see p. 100).

No single strategy works for all situations, and sometimes learners need to use multiple strategies to figure out a word. The more strategies a person knows, the more likely it is that the person can recognize words successfully. Activities #32–39 help teach these strategies. The strategies can be taught in any order. Start by building on what the learner already knows.

Sight words

Words that learners recognize instantly without having to stop to figure them out. The more proficient readers are, the more words they recognize by sight.

Phonics

The use of sound-symbol relationships to decode words.

Word patterns

The use of familiar letter groupings to help recognize parts of words.

Context

The use of the surrounding words to help figure out an unfamiliar word.

Word parts

The use of root words, suffixes, prefixes, and other word parts to recognize a word.

Purpose

To help learners recognize as many words as possible by sight in order to improve reading speed and comprehension

How

1. Work with the learners to choose the words they want to learn. Examples:

   - words they will be using often in daily life or words from their language experience stories (see Activity #28)

   - words that appear often in general writing, such as *the, there, this,* and *was*

   - words with irregular spellings that are difficult to sound out phonetically, such as *height*

   - survival words, such as family names or words that appear on forms and applications, on job-related materials, on road signs, or in public places

2. Ask each learner to print the selected words on index cards. (You can help if needed.) Make a set of cards for yourself.

3. If a learner has trouble remembering a word, ask him or her to use the new word in a sentence. Write the sentence. Ask the learner to copy the sentence on the back of the flash card. You can also ask the learner to draw a picture of the word on the back of the card.

4. Show each card (from your own set) and ask the learners to read it.

5. Encourage the learners to review their own flash cards at home.

6. Review the words often.

Suggestions

- Take the time to teach these words orally to ensure that the learners know their meaning before you teach them as sight words.

- Teach no more than 6 to 10 new words at a time. Use fewer cards if the learners have problems with that many.

- Periodically ask each learner to read the cards and divide them into two piles: those the learner knows and those he or she still has difficulty with. Work with the learner to reduce the size of the second pile.

- Set a specific amount of time. Ask the learners to read as many cards as possible in that time. Repeat the exercise to show improvement.

- Talk about any new words, or ask the learners to use each word in a sentence. This enables the learners to develop a fuller context for the word, which helps both with oral skills and with the ability to recognize the word in print.

- See Appendix C in *Teaching Adults: A Literacy Resource Book* (published by New Readers Press) for a list of the 300 most frequently used words.

Activity 33 Phonics: Teaching Consonant Sounds

Purpose

To enable learners to decode unfamiliar words by using knowledge of the sound-letter relationships

How

1. From the reading selection or the learners' language experience stories select two or three words that begin with the same consonant and sound.

2. Ask the learners to write each word on a piece of paper and underline the initial consonant.

3. Ask the learners to name the letter. Teach it if necessary.

4. Say the sound of the letter, and ask the learners to repeat after you.

5. Ask for examples of other words that start with that sound, or give examples yourself.

6. Write these words on paper. Say the sound as you underline the letter at the beginning of the word. (Be careful not to use words that start with the same letter if the letter has a different sound in each word. Examples: *park, phone.*)

7. Have the learners practice identifying the same initial sound in other words that they know.

8. If one of the learners needs help remembering a sound, ask him or her to choose a key word that will help. Examples: *car* for /c/, *hand* for /h/.

Suggestions

- Use the same technique to teach consonant blends *(st, scr)* and digraphs *(sh)*.

  digraph: A group of two letters that express one sound. Example: *sh.*

  consonant blend: Two or three consonants that are pronounced almost as one sound. Examples: *pl, str.* You hear the sound of each letter.

- After the learners can identify consonant sounds at the beginning of words, repeat the process to teach consonant sounds at the end and in the middle of words.

- Review sounds taught in previous lessons.

- For an idea on how to use minimal pairs to help learners distinguish between frequently confused vowel or consonant sounds, see Activity #24.

- For additional information on teaching consonant and vowel sounds, see the *Laubach Way to English* series (described in Appendix A).

- For assistance in describing individual sounds, see pp. 78–80 and Appendix B.

 Activity 34 — Phonics: The Disappearing Person

Purpose

To provide a fun way to help learners use sounds to figure out a word

How

1. Pick a word the learners know.

2. On a piece of paper or a chalkboard, draw short horizontal lines, one for each letter in the word.

3. Draw a stick figure next to the lines (in pencil if you are using paper). See the sample on p. 104.

4. Ask one of the learners to guess a letter.

5. If the letter is used in the word, write it on the appropriate line (or lines). If not, write the letter at the top of the paper and erase one of the stick figure's body parts (hand, foot, leg, arm, or head).

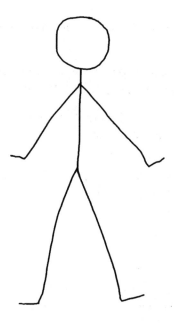

6. Repeat step 5, giving each learner in the group a chance to guess a letter.

7. The learners win by guessing the word before you erase the last part of the figure (the body).

8. Ask one of the learners to take a turn at picking a word and leading the activity.

Suggestions

- If you are working with a large group, divide the learners into two teams.

- Select words that contain sounds the learners need to practice.

Word Patterns

Purpose

To help learners recognize new words more quickly without having to sound out and blend each individual sound in the word

How

1. Make sure the learners understand the concept of rhyming. Say several pairs of words and ask if they rhyme.

Teaching Adults: An ESL Resource Book

2. Choose a word pattern with which you can create several rhyming words. Example: *-it*.

3. Write the word pattern at the top of a piece of paper and ask the learner to say the sound. If no one knows the sound, say it yourself. Example

4. Below the pattern write a word that ends in that pattern. Example: *sit*. (Throughout the activity, use words the learners know orally.) Ask the learners what the word is. If they don't know, read it yourself.

5. Write a word that rhymes with the first word (and has a different initial consonant). Example: *bit*. Ask the learners to read it. If they have difficulty, give a hint: "If *s-i-t* is *sit,* then what is *b-i-t?*"

6. Keep adding words and asking the learners to read them.

7. Ask the learners to add other words using the same pattern. If they have difficulty coming up with words, offer some of your own. Take the time to teach the meaning of the words. Note that a learner might create a word that is not a real word in English. If that happens, explain that this is the case, but compliment the person on his or her understanding of the concepts of patterns and rhyming.

8. Ask the learners to read through the entire list.

   Example:

   -it
   sit
   bit
   fit
   hit
   lit
   flit

Suggestions

- This recognition strategy can also be helpful for figuring out multisyllabic words as learners try to identify the pattern in each syllable.

   -ar   -et
   tar   get

   target

- Do not confuse beginning learners by using ending sounds that can be spelled more than one way. Examples: *fix* and *picks, tax* and *stacks*.

- When the learners are comfortable with a pattern, dictate other words that have the same pattern and ask the learners to write them.

ee Appendix H in *Teaching Adults: A Literacy Resource Book* (published by New Readers Press) for examples of common word patterns.

- You can make flash cards, one for the pattern and one for each beginning letter(s). The learner can put the pattern card together with the other cards to create various new words. He or she can then read the new words aloud.

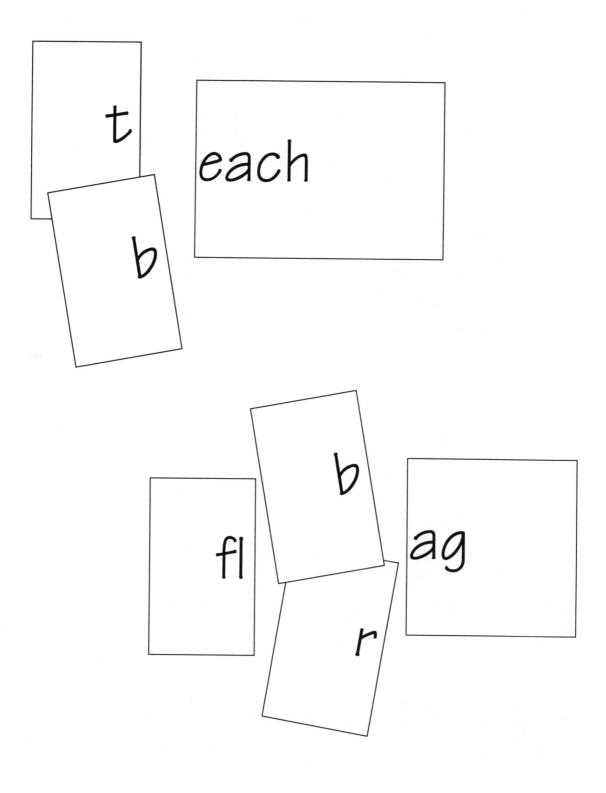

- You can fold an index card and cut a window in one side of it to make a "word slide." Tape the top and bottom of the card together, and write the word ending next to the window. On a separate card, write the beginning letters that you want to work on. The learner can pull this card through the word slide and read each new word as the letters appear in the window.

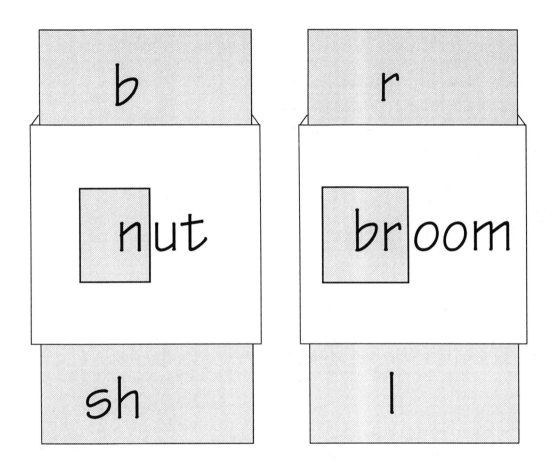

Context: Just Say "Blank"

Purpose

To encourage a learner to continue reading when the learner comes to a word he or she doesn't know and to return to the word later with more information (context) to figure it out

How

1. When the learner comes to a word he or she doesn't recognize, tell the learner to just say "blank" and keep reading.

2. Encourage the learner to use the rest of the sentence or paragraph to come up with a word that would make sense in that place (is logical, has meaning, and is grammatically appropriate).

3. If there is more than one possibility, ask the learner to see if the first sound in the word helps narrow down the choices. Example: A learner doesn't recognize the word *paid* in the following sentence. *Sam paid twenty dollars for the tickets.* From the context, the learner figures that the word could be *spent, paid,* or *gave.* From the first sound in the word, the learner realizes the word cannot be *spent* or *gave.*

4. Ask the learner to read the complete sentence aloud.

Activity 37   Context: CLOZE Procedure

Purpose

To help learners practice using context—the meaning of surrounding words and sentences—to fill in missing words in a sentence or paragraph. (The word *CLOZE* comes from *closure* and means finishing or "closing" a sentence.)

How

1. Select a passage that is at or below the learners' current reading level. Leave the first sentence intact. For beginning readers, delete approximately every 10th word. (You can make this exercise more challenging by deleting more words, e.g., every fifth word.) The following example deletes every fifth word:

    > Every day I went to look in the bird's nest. Yesterday there were four _____ in the nest. The _____ wasn't there. When she _____ back, she quickly hopped _____ the nest and sat _____ the eggs.

2. Ask the learners to take turns reading the sentences and filling in the missing words.

Suggestions

- If you want to make this activity easier, you can provide a word list for the learners to choose from. Or you can write the first letter of the word on the line to serve as a clue.

- Remind the learners to choose words that make sense in context. Unless they are working from a word list, they do not need to write a particular word. There may be more than one option.

- Use material with which the learners are already familiar, such as a language experience story or a passage from a previous lesson.

- If the material is new, give the learners an overview of the contents before they start reading.

- If the learners have difficulty writing, ask them to write only the first letter of the word or to say the word while you write it.

- As a follow-up activity, you can go back and ask the learners to explain why they selected these particular words.

Activity 38 Word Parts: Compound Words

Purpose

To help learners put words together to form compound words

How

1. Select five or six compound words that are made up of smaller words that the learners can already read.

2. Write the first part of each word in one column (on a chalkboard or large piece of paper).

3. Write the second part of each word in a second column. Do not put them in the same order as in the first column.

4. Ask one of the learners to draw a line that connects a word in the first column to a word in the second column, forming a compound word. Have the learner read the new word aloud.

5. If you're not sure that the learner recognizes the word, ask the learner to use it in a sentence.

6. Give each learner a chance to find and read a compound word.

Example:

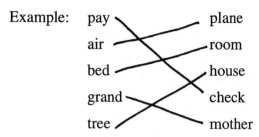

pay   plane
air   room
bed   house
grand   check
tree   mother

Activity 39

Word Parts: Changing Root Words

Purpose

To help learners understand how adding a prefix or suffix can change the meaning of a root word

How

1. On the chalkboard write five or six words that have both a prefix and a suffix. These should be words that the learners already know orally.

2. Ask one of the learners to go up to the board and to underline the prefix and circle the suffix in the first word.

   Examples:

   <u>un</u>interest(ed)

   <u>non</u>tradition(al)

3. Ask the learner to use the root word in a sentence. Write the sentence, or ask the learner to write it.

4. Ask the learner to use the root word with the suffix in a sentence. Write the sentence.

5. Ask the learner to use the word with both the prefix and the suffix in a sentence. Write the sentence.

6. Discuss how adding the prefix and suffix changed the meaning of the word.

7. Have different learners from the group do the same with the remaining words.

Developing Fluent Oral Reading

Many ESL learners who do not read English well are unsure of themselves and read haltingly, with little or no expression. This can be the case even if they have already learned the vocabulary words orally. They often pause and wait for the tutor to tell them how they're doing. Such learners need to develop confidence and learn how to read fluently because fluent reading will improve their ability to understand and enjoy what they read. In addition, some learners have a specific goal that requires oral reading, such as reading stories to children or reading religious texts aloud.

Three oral techniques for teaching reading are listed below. These techniques are described in Activities #40–42. The first technique provides the most support for the learner: The learner listens as you read aloud. The next two techniques are designed to increase learner independence to the point at which the learner is reading alone.

Reading to the learner: Learner listens as tutor reads.

Duet reading: Tutor and learner read together.

Echo reading: Tutor reads first and then learner reads same sentence or paragraph.

Activity 40   Reading Aloud to the Learner

Purposes

- To allow the learner to hear someone read with good expression and phrasing

- To enable the learner to use materials that are too hard to read independently

- To allow the learner to practice listening to English that will be somewhat challenging for him or her to understand

- To enable the tutor to share with the learner materials that the tutor has found interesting, thus exposing the learner to possible new ideas and building the tutor/learner relationship

- To provide a change of pace in the lesson

How

1. Select a short passage or text that you know will be of interest to the learner. Be sure that the learner will know the meaning of most of the words. (But the learner will not have to be able to read the material.)

2. Tell the learner that you are going to read aloud. Ask the learner to tell you if he or she does not understand something as you read.

3. Have the learner either follow along in a copy of the material or sit next to you and look at your reading selection.

4. Read aloud to the learner.

Suggestions

- You may want to discuss the selection's subject matter beforehand to ensure that the learner is capable of understanding most of what you will be reading. Teach orally any vocabulary that may be new for the learner.

- It is more important for the learner to hear you read than to follow along word by word in the passage. If the learner becomes frustrated over losing the place while trying to follow along, ask the learner just to listen.

Duet Reading

Purpose

To give practice in fluent reading without putting the learner on the spot to read difficult material alone. Duet reading also helps the ESL learner

- pay attention to punctuation marks
- develop good eye movement in order to keep the place
- read words in natural phrases
- learn new sight words
- read with expression
- read for enjoyment

How

(Use duet reading after the learner develops some basic sight vocabulary.)

1. Choose something that is a little too hard for the learner.

   Collect several books, magazine or newspaper articles, pamphlets, or brochures that address topics of interest to the learner and that are somewhat above his or her current reading level. Ask the learner to select which piece to read.

2. Begin reading together.

   Sit next to the learner and read aloud together from the same selection. Read at a normal speed, using expression and observing punctuation. The learner reads along, trying to keep up with you.

3. Use your finger.

   Move your finger beneath the line as you read to help the learner keep up.

4. Keep going.

   Continue to read at a normal rate even if the learner hesitates or falls behind. Stop if the learner stops reading completely.

5. Don't ask questions.

   Do not ask any questions to check the learner's understanding. Do not stop to explain the meaning of a word unless the learner asks. This material is to be used only as an oral reading exercise.

6. Decide if the reading material is too hard or too easy.

   If the learner keeps up easily, select more challenging material. If the material seems too difficult, use something that may be easier because it is written more simply or because the learner knows more about the subject.

Suggestions

- Use duet reading only for brief periods (7 to 10 minutes).

- Don't ask learners to read aloud from the material by themselves. Since the material is above their independent reading level, that could be a frustrating experience.

- If you use duet reading at the beginning of a lesson, reread part of the same selection with the learner before the end of the lesson. Then the learner can see how much easier it gets with practice.

- You can also use this technique with the learner's own writing or with stories that are at the learner's level to practice fluent reading.

Purpose

To provide support by first modeling the reading before asking the learner to read it aloud independently

How

1. Select material that is somewhat above the learner's independent reading level.

2. Check to make sure the learner understands the key vocabulary before you begin reading.

3. For a beginning reader, read each sentence aloud and then ask the learner to read it aloud. For a more advanced reader, model each paragraph instead of each sentence.

4. Encourage the learner to try reading independently as soon as he or she is comfortable doing so.

Suggestions

- After you both have read several sentences (or paragraphs), you could ask the learner to read the entire section again.

- You can also use this strategy with material at the learner's reading level if the learner needs help reading fluently.

- Make audiotapes of the reading selections so the learner can practice reading aloud at home. You can also use books that have accompanying read-along audiotapes, available from various publishers. (For examples of materials sold by New Readers Press, see Appendix A.)

Getting Started with Writing

Since many ESL learners will be unfamiliar with the Roman alphabet, you might have to begin by teaching people how to write the letters. In most cases, it is best to start with printing (sometimes called "manuscript writing") rather than with cursive writing.

Activity #43 can be used to teach learners to write the letters of the alphabet.

When learners can do this comfortably, you can encourage them to copy words and sentences. This will help the learners develop a sense of the proper spacing to use between letters and words, when to use capital letters, and where to place punctuation marks. An excellent place to start with copying is by having learners copy all or part of their own language experience stories. See Activity #28.

Other useful activities for developing basic writing skills include

- making lists (of family members, groceries to buy, chores to do, bills to pay, jobs the learner has held)

- writing appointments, birthdays, or other special occasions on a calendar

- filling out sample forms (job applications, checks, medical forms)

- writing entries in an address book

- writing words on flash cards to learn as sight words

- creating a personal dictionary of words the learner wants to remember or uses often

 Activity 43 Letter Formation: Five Steps to Printing

Purpose

To teach printing to learners who do not write in any language or who are unfamiliar with the Roman alphabet

How

1. Select a word from a reading selection that contains the letter the learner wants to work on. Read the word and review the name and sound of the letter if necessary.

2. First demonstrate each stroke needed to print the letter. Make the strokes in the air. Then ask the learner to do it with you.

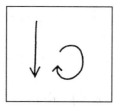

3. Make the strokes on unlined paper. Then ask the learner to copy them.

4. Write the whole letter on unlined paper. Describe the letter as you make it. Then ask the learner to print the letter.

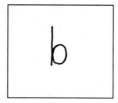

5. Write the letter on lined paper. Use paper with three guidelines. Explain that all letters stand on the bottom guideline. Some letters start from the top guideline and some from the middle guideline. Some letters descend below the bottom line. Then print the letter on the guidelines and ask the learner to trace it.

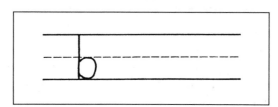

6. Ask the learner to use a pencil to practice printing the same letter several times on the guidelines.

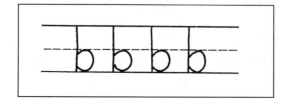

Suggestions

- Teach only the letters the learner does not know.

- Whenever possible, link the writing to the reading.

- It isn't necessary to teach the letters in alphabetical order. You might help the learner learn to print the letters in his or her name first. You can also ask if there are letters the learner would like to start with.

- Make sure the learner has plenty of room on the table and that the chair and table are at a comfortable height. Be sure there is enough light as well.

- Provide a pencil with an eraser. Many learners do not like to leave mistakes or have messy papers. The pencil will be easier to use if it has a somewhat dull point, because new writers tend to exert a lot of pressure.

- Limit writing practice for beginners to prevent hand fatigue or cramps. Limit the number of new letters you introduce in each lesson.

- Keep a sample printing chart (see pp. 118–119) on the table for reference until the learner can write all the letters and numbers independently.

- If the learner is having a lot of difficulty remembering the shape of the letter, ask him or her to describe the shape and relate it to a familiar object as a memory "key."

    Examples: *O* is round like an orange, *J* looks like a fishhook.

- You can adapt this process to teach cursive writing after the learner is comfortable and proficient with printing.

- Letters can look very different depending on the typeface used. To help the learner recognize letters of the alphabet in different typefaces, select examples from magazines or newspapers. Cut them out and paste them on sheets of paper, a separate sheet for each letter. As an alternative, ask the learner to find and cut out his or her own examples.

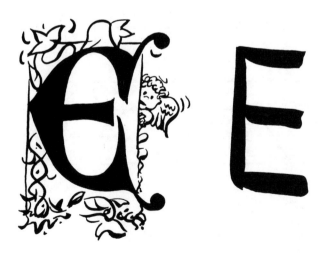

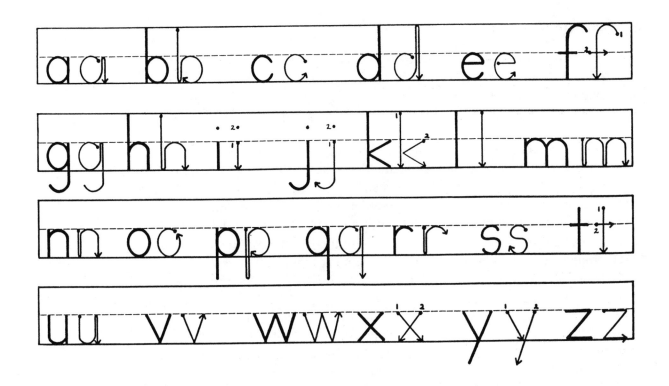

Sample Cursive Writing Chart

Guided Writing

When ESL learners are able to write the letters of the alphabet and copy words and sentences or write them from dictation, they are ready to begin creating their own text—using writing to share their own ideas and experiences.

But at this stage, beginning ESL learners often approach writing as a grueling task. They worry about making grammatical mistakes, mispelling words, or writing something that no one will understand. They often view writing as an agonizing act of creating something in order for the teacher or tutor to correct it. As a result, they become overly concerned with the technical aspect of writing—of getting it "right." They lose sight of the fact that writing is a tool to communicate ideas. Because of this, they don't see themselves as writers, and they fail to appreciate all the strengths they bring to the writing process.

By urging beginning writers to focus on meaning rather than correctness, you can help them overcome their fear of writing. Activities #44–45 help the learners get started with writing sentences. Activities #46–47 share ideas for getting learners started down the path of independent writing. All are "guided writing" activities because *you* decide the topic and develop a controlled structure that allows people to express their ideas without having to struggle unnecessarily.

Activities #46–47 also involve collaborative or interactive writing. In Activity #46, you and the learner collaborate on a writing project. In Activity #47, a group of learners work together on a project. For learners who have had little writing experience, collaborating with others can help build confidence *and* ability.

Collaborative writing is especially useful with multi-level groups. Each learner contributes at his or her ability level, and all share equally in the success of the final product. A learner who has never written more than a sentence or two can still feel proud of having made an important contribution to a much longer piece of writing.

Because group members share the responsibility for the task, the stress that often accompanies writing lessons is greatly reduced. Learners are free to focus on what they're saying, and to enjoy the creative process. They will find their own ideas stimulated by reading and hearing the ideas of the others in the group. Finally, the fun and creativity that develop during collaborative activities often carry over to other writing tasks, and help make learners more willing to tackle writing in general.

Guided Writing: Sentence Completion with Pictures

Purpose

To use pictures as a stimulus to help learners complete sentences and generate sentences of their own

How

1. Select a picture or photograph and either show it on an overhead projector or make photocopies and distribute one to each learner. The picture should be one that includes vocabulary that the learners are familiar with.

2. Learners can work in pairs or individually, depending on their ability.

3. Tell the learners that this is a writing activity. Explain that you will start to tell them sentences about the picture. Their job will be to finish the sentences. You can make the sentence frames as easy or as difficult as you feel is appropriate. Read the sentence frames aloud to the learners. Some examples:

    The man is _____.

    The tree is big and _____.

    The woman looks very _____.

    The policeman is trying to _____.

    No one is noticing that _____.

4. Call on a few learners to read their sentences. Discuss their answers with the whole group.

Suggestion

As the learners become familiar with this activity, move on to a more advanced variation. Show a picture and ask questions about the picture. Have the learners write their answers to the questions. Remind the learners to form complete sentences as they write. Some examples:

    Why is everyone staring at the man?
    Where did he find that unusual hat?
    Would you like to have a hat like that? Why?

(Adapted from a presentation by Sharon Miller and Jill DeGrange.)

Activity

45 Guided Writing: Prompted Sentences

Purpose

To teach learners to write some simple sentences based on one topic sentence

How

1. Tell the learners that you will help them write a few sentences.

2. Tell them to write a complete sentence about three things they brought with them to class today.

3. After they have done this, tell them to describe the first item in writing:

    "What does it look like?"
    "What is it used for?"
    "How long have you had it?"

    If necessry, help the learners put their thoughts into complete sentences. For example, if a learner brings in a pencil and responds to the first question by writing "a stick," show them that they should write something like "The pencil looks like a stick."

4. Continue to ask similar questions about the other two items.

5. When everyone is finished, call on learners to read their short paragraphs to the rest of the group. Invite the group to ask the writer questions about what he or she has written.

Suggestions

*   Although you will be encouraging the learners to write complete sentences to answer your questions, do not be concerned if the sentences are not grammatically correct. The goal is for the learners to begin to string together some sentences that flow from one topic sentence.

*   You can set up this activity in a number of different ways. Some other prompts to use to help learners put together a short paragraph include the following:

    "Write a sentence that tells me what kind of weekend you had."

    Follow-up questions to ask (for learners to write more sentences):

    "Why was it this kind of weekend?"
    "Did you expect the weekend to turn out as it did? Why or why not?"

122

Teaching Adults: An ESL Resource Book

"Write a sentence that tells me about what you do in your spare time."

Follow-up questions to ask (for learners to write more sentences):

"Why do you like to do this?"
"When did you become interested in it?"
"How did you start doing it?"

(Adapted from a presentation by Sharon Miller and Jill DeGrange.)

Activity 46 Guided Writing: Using Pictures in One-to-One Tutoring

Purpose

To support the beginning learner in writing original sentences in response to questions about a picture chosen by the tutor

How

1. Show the learner a picture, photograph, or drawing depicting one person.

2. Ask the learner to think about the person in the picture.

3. Ask a question about the picture. ("What's the person's name?") Explain that there are no "right" answers to the questions you will be asking in this activity. The learner can make up any answer, but the answer must be in a complete sentence. Have the learner answer orally. ("Her name is Anna.")

4. Give the learner a piece of paper and tell him or her to write the answer. Explain that the learner need not be concerned about correct spelling or grammar at this point.

5. Ask a second question that builds on the learner's first answer. ("Where does Anna live?") Have the learner answer orally (in a complete sentence).

6. Tell the learner to write the answer below the answer to the first question.

7. Continue asking questions that build on the learner's previous response. (You might have to look at the learner's paper to see what the previous response was.) The following is an example of how such a guided writing activity might proceed.

Tutor	Learner
What's the person's name?	Her name is Anna.
Where does Anna live?	She lives in Los Angeles.
Who does she live with?	She lives with her mother, father, and two sisters.
How old is she?	She is 18 years old.
How does she feel about her life?	She is very happy.
Why is she happy?	She's happy because she won $100,000 in the lottery.
What is she going to do with all that money?	She is going to buy a new house, and she will go to college.
Why does she want to go to college?	She wants to be a lawyer.

8. Ask the learner to read aloud the sentences he or she wrote.

Suggestions

- You can reuse the same picture in a later lesson. The story can always be different. To make sure that the story will be different, change your first question.

- It is important to avoid questions that can be answered with a yes-or-no response. Otherwise, the learner might end up with a story that reads as follows:

Tutor	Learner
What's the person's name?	Her name is Anna.
Does Anna live in the country?	No.
Does she live in a city?	Yes.
What city does she live in?	She lives in Los Angeles.

- It is important to have the learner form complete sentences so that the story will read like a real story, e.g., "She is 18 years old," not "18 years old."

(Adapted from a presentation given by Sharron Bassano.)

Guided Writing: Using Pictures with Small Groups

Purpose

To enable learners to participate in the writing of several stories without the pressure of having to create a whole story themselves

How

This activity works best with a small group of five or six learners. The directions below are for a group of five.

1. Collect five different magazine or newspaper pictures that depict just one person. Each person in the group will need a different picture. (If you are working with several groups, you can use multiple copies of one picture as long as you don't give the same picture to people in the same group.)

2. Give each learner a picture with a blank sheet of paper taped or stapled to the back of it.

3. Ask the learners to look at their pictures and imagine who the person is and what the person's background and life are like.

4. Write the first set of questions on a chalkboard where each member of the group can see them. Read the questions aloud. Example:

   a) What is his/her name?
   How old is he/she?
   What does he/she do?

5. Ask the learners to turn their pictures over and write the answers to these questions (using complete sentences) on the attached piece of paper. Tell them not to worry about correct spelling or grammar. Encourage them to be as imaginative about the person in the picture as they want to be.

6. When they have finished writing, have them pass the picture to the person on the right. (The activity will be easier if the learners are seated in a circle or around a table.)

7. Ask each learner to look at the new picture, turn it over, and read the sentences written by the previous learner.

8. Write the following set of questions on the chalkboard. Read them aloud.

   b) Where does he/she live?
   Who does he/she live with?

9. Ask the learners to write the answers to these questions on the sheet of paper they are now holding. Remind them that they are writing about the person in the new picture and that they can be as creative as they want to be in their answers.

10. When they finish writing, ask each learner to again pass the picture to the right. Repeat steps 7–9 for each of the following questions or sets of questions.

   c) What does he/she like to do?
      What doesn't he/she like to do?

   d) What did he/she do yesterday? Why?

   e) What is he/she going to do tomorrow?

11. When the learners have answered all the questions, ask each person to pass the picture to the right one more time. Everyone should have his/her original picture plus a story containing segments written by each member of the group. The resulting stories are usually quite entertaining.

12. At this point, have the learners hold up their pictures and read "their" stories to the other members of their group.

Suggestions

- If you are working with groups smaller than five, you can either set up a shorter writing task (fewer sets of questions) or you can instruct learners to keep passing their pictures around until the task is finished—even though they will then be working on some of the stories twice.

- If you have to work with larger groups, simply "add to the plot" by providing additional sets of questions.

- Allow enough time for the learners to look at each new picture and to read the previously written sentences.

- Although everyone in the group contributed equally to each of the stories, the person who started the picture story usually feels some "ownership" for that story, so it's best if the story winds up back with that person at the end.

- You can design the questions in such a way as to encourage learners to write about a specific topic that the group is studying. Examples: occupations, going to the doctor or some other health issue, shopping, or moving into a new apartment or house.

- You can simplify this activity for beginning-level learners by providing sentence frames for the learners to complete. With this added control, the learners will feel more comfortable and be better able to focus on their contribution to the story. You can write the sentence frames on a chalkboard for learners to copy. Or you can make photocopies and attach one set to the back of each picture. Examples of sentence frames:

1) This is _____.

   He is _____ years old.

   He lives in _____ with _____.

2) He likes _____, but he doesn't like _____.

3) Yesterday he _____ because _____.

4) He used to be _____, but now he is _____.

5) Tomorrow he will _____.

(Adapted from a presentation by Louis Spaventa.)

Free Writing

As learners get ready for more independent or "free" writing, they may still need help developing their ideas or organizing their thoughts. Activities #48–49 represent two ways to help learners decide what they want to write about. At this more advanced stage, it's still important to focus on meaning and on effective communication without being overly concerned about correctness. Both of these activities are designed to "prime the pump"—to enable learners at all levels to get their ideas on paper before they begin to write.

The remaining activities in this section encourage the learners to be more creative and take greater responsibility for deciding what they want to write and how. This is the time to help learners realize that good writers seldom create a finished piece on their first try; they often do a first "rough" draft and then several revisions as they try to make their ideas clear and complete.

Again, the focus in the draft stage should be on meaning and content. Remind learners not to worry about spelling or grammar. Once the learners are satisfied with the content, they can work on editing or "correcting" the writing.

Activity 48 Free Writing: Semantic Webs

Purpose

To enable beginning writers to organize their thoughts about a topic before they begin to write

How

1. Tell the learners you are going to show them something that will help them get started with their writing—something called a "web" or sometimes a "mind map."

2. Explain that they will first help *you* make a web. Later they will have a chance to make their own.

3. Tell the learners that you want to write something about winter. You have lots of ideas, but do not know where to start.

4. Write the word *winter* in a circle in the middle of the chalkboard.

5. Ask what the learners think about when they think of winter. Develop a semantic web using their ideas. Example:

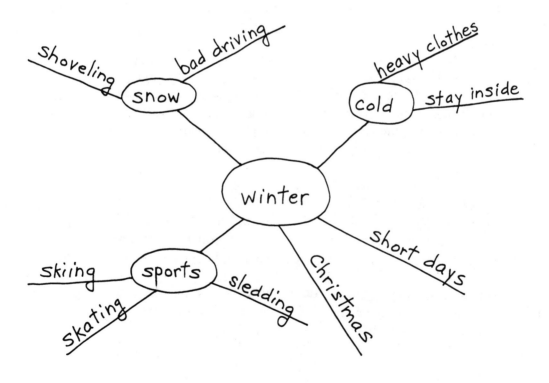

6. When the web is complete, ask the learners to pick a portion of the web and use it to make up some sentences about winter. Provide help as necessary.

   Examples of things they might say:

   > "I wear heavy clothes in winter."
   > "I like stay inside when cold."

   If the learners' sentences are not grammatically correct, don't make corrections unless another learner in the group points out the error. In that event, you should make the correction since other learners in the group may become confused if you don't. But first give the learner who provided the sentence an opportunity to tell you how the sentence could be corrected.

7. Write the sentences on the chalkboard in the sequence that the learners say them. Do not be concerned if the sentences don't seem to relate to each other.

8. After the learners have generated several sentences, tell them to pick another portion of the web and create a second group of sentences. Write these on the chalkboard.

9. Hand out to each learner a 3" x 5" card with a different word written on each. Give each learner a large piece of paper and ask him or her to develop a web from that one word. Encourage the learners to have fun.

10. Circulate among the learners as they work on their webs. Help them think of things related to their topic. Guide them in deciding what the subtopics should be.

11. After the learners have had sufficient time to develop their webs, ask them to write a few sentences from the web. (You may want to have learners develop the webs in one class and then write the sentences in the next class.)

Suggestions

- During your initial demonstration, you will have to help the learners draw connections and see possible subtopics. For example, if learners talk about skiing, ice skating, and sledding, ask what they could call all these things ("sports"). Then write this subtopic in a circle with a line from it to the center circle and other lines from it to the specific examples. This may require some practice on your part. As the learners see the relationships, they might decide to add more examples.

- Help learners who are struggling with the English words they need to express their ideas. Be prepared to stop and teach any new vocabulary that comes up.

- When asking learners to do this activity for the first time on their own, it may be easier to have them work in pairs rather than individually.

- After the individual or pair work is done, you can have the entire group work together to create sentences for each of the completed webs.

Learners who are uncertain about their ability will feel less pressured if they don't each have to create the sentences on their own.

- You can vary the activity by using two webs to generate sentences that compare and contrast. For example, you might want learners to write a report about a field trip you took together. You can make the task easier by asking them to first create two webs: "What I liked" and "What I did not like."

Activity 49 Free Writing: Five-Minute Warm-up

Purpose

To provide an unstructured opportunity for learners to capture their ideas through sustained writing in preparation for creating a first draft

How

1. Ask the learners to take out a pen and several sheets of paper.

2. Work with the group to select a topic, or pick a topic that you think would be of interest to them.

3. Give each learner five minutes to write everything he or she knows about this topic.

4. Emphasize that they do not have to write complete sentences; nor should they worry about correct grammar, spelling, or punctuation. No one else will read what they write. Later they will use this writing to create a first draft about something related to this topic.

5. Encourage the learners to write whatever pops into their heads and not spend a lot of time thinking about it. Just keep writing!

6. After the five minutes are up, give each person a couple of minutes to read over what he or she has written.

7. Divide the learners into pairs. Ask them to work together to share the ideas they wrote about.

Suggestion

After this sharing, you might need to ask some of the learners to narrow the topic by selecting only a part of what they wrote as the basis for the rough draft they will create.

Activity 50   Free Writing: Group Storytelling

Purpose

To provide oral and written practice in story development

How

1. Seat all the learners in a circle.

2. Explain that you want each person to help create a story. Afterward, they will do some writing.

3. Start the story yourself. Talk about anything that involves people doing something. After about 30 seconds, point to the learner on your right and ask that person to continue the story for about 30 seconds. Tell the learner that he or she should have fun and not worry about how the story goes. Emphasize that there is no correct way to create the story.

4. After 30 seconds, signal for the next person to continue the story.

5. Depending on the size of the group, give everyone one to three turns to contribute to the story.

6. After the story is fairly well developed, stop and ask each learner to write for a few minutes to continue the story. Tell them not to worry if they do not finish the story. Also, they should not worry about making mistakes; their goal is to continue telling the story in writing as they did just now by speaking.

7. After they have had several minutes to write, call on individual learners to read aloud what they have written.

Activity 51 — Free Writing: "I Like to Eat Chocolate"

Purpose

To help learners understand how to write paragraphs

How

1. On a sheet of paper list the numbers 1–10 down the left-hand side. Next to each number write the same sentence:

    I like _____ because _____.

2. Give a copy of this to each learner.

3. Ask each person to try to complete all 10 sentences, listing different things that they like and why. Give them examples such as:

    "I like pumpkin pie because it tastes sweet."
    "I like to listen to music because it relaxes me."

4. Tell the learners not to be concerned about getting the grammar, spelling, or punctuation correct. They can work on these things later. For now, they should simply enjoy the creative process.

5. After they have completed some or all or several of the sentences (completing them all is not important), call on two or three learners to share one of their sentences with everyone. Tell them they do not have to read from their paper. If they want, they can just tell everyone, in their own words, what they like or like to do and why.

6. Explain that you would like each of the learners to select one of their own sentences and write a paragraph based on that sentence.

7. Write the definition of a paragraph on a flip chart or the chalkboard:

    A paragraph is a group of sentences that are put together because all the sentences are about one topic.

8. Write the following sentence on the board. Or use one of the sentences written by a learner.

    I like to eat chocolate because it tastes great.

9. Explain that this will be the topic sentence for the sample paragraph. Write this definition on the board:

    A topic sentence indicates what the rest of the paragraph will be about.

10. Explain that the other sentences in the paragraph will give the reasons, explanations, or further details about the topic sentence.

11. Show how this works by leading the group in developing a paragraph based on the sentence you wrote on the board. Encourage the learners to help you by suggesting additional sentences.

12. After you have a few sentences on the chalkboard, read the paragraph.

13. At this point, do some initial revising as a model for the learners. For example, you might add or delete a word or two or rearrange the sentences so they are in a more logical order. Explain that you are still looking at meaning and are not trying to correct any "mistakes."

14. Ask each of the learners to select one of their own sentences and write a short paragraph that starts with that sentence. Remind them not to worry about correctness. Tell them they can write whatever they want. (They might provide more information about why they like something. Or they might develop a funny story.) Encourage them to enjoy their writing.

15. Emphasize that the learners *will not* have to share their writing with anybody but you.

Suggestions

- For additional practice, ask learners to write another paragraph using a different sentence.

- Ask more advanced students to try to write a whole story made up of several paragraphs, each based on one of the topic sentences.

(Taken from Tana Reiff, *Writing Me! A First Writing Course for Adults,* © 1978 by New Readers Press. Used by permission.)

 Activity 52 Free Writing: Writing with Partners

Purposes

- To help learners develop a sense of "audience"—who they are writing for

- To provide practice in giving feedback about another person's writing

- To help learners utilize another person's feedback when deciding how to revise their own writing

How

Introduce the activity

1. Tell the learners you want to show them a way to write on a specific topic. This may be a new way for them to write. Tell them this is meant to be an enjoyable experience. They should relax and have fun.

Select a topic

2. Tell the learners to pick any topic they'd like to write about. (The first time you do this activity you may want to have all the learners write on the same topic.)

Develop a shared knowledge base

3. This step will be necessary only if you have required the learners to all write on the same topic. If so, lead a group discussion on the topic as a pre-writing activity to ensure that everyone has an adequate knowledge base from which to write.

Begin writing

4. Ask the learners to begin writing on the topic. Tell them not to be concerned at this point with grammar, spelling, choice of words, punctuation, how it sounds, or who will read it. Explain that they should concentrate on getting their ideas down on paper.

5. If you are doing this activity for the first time, model step 4 for the learners. Ask them to watch while you begin to write. Pick a different topic and use a chalkboard or overhead transparency so everyone can see. Write freely and put your thoughts down as they come into your mind. Again, don't be concerned with correct grammar, spelling, or anything else except the process of writing down your thoughts. Don't correct anything as you go.

Create a first draft

6. Tell the learners to think of a close friend or relative.

7. Ask them to write a letter to this person explaining or describing something about the topic. They can choose any aspect of the topic. Remind them again to write freely and not be concerned with correctness.

Share your work

8. Tell the learners that you will ask each of them to work with a partner to help improve what they have written.

9. Explain that you will begin by reading aloud a sample of your own writing. (This should be short—one page or less.) Explain that the learners should

- listen as you read

- make a praise statement after you finish reading: say one good thing about the writing

- ask one or two questions that they want you to answer: either to clarify something they didn't understand or to ask for more information on the topic

10. Model this process for the learners.

- Read your piece to them.

- When you finish, ask for a volunteer to make a praise statement.

- Then ask other volunteers for questions. Answer their questions.

11. Put the learners in pairs.

12. Tell them to take turns reading their letters slowly to each other. After the first person finishes reading, the partner makes a praise statement and asks one or two questions (either for clarification or more information). After the reader answers the questions, both learners should feel free to further discuss what the first person wrote.

13. Give a signal for the pair to change roles and for the second person to read his or her letter. Repeat step 12.

Revise the writing

14. Ask the learners to think about their discussions, decide what they'd like to change in their letters based on these discussions, and then rewrite the letters to incorporate these changes.

Edit the writing

15. When learners are satisfied with their revisions, you can work with them to begin editing the pieces—or making them "correct." When you start this process, ask them to focus on only one thing at a time. For example, if you have worked in class on capital letters, you can ask them to check their work to make sure that every sentence begins with a capital letter.

Suggestions

- If the learners are having difficulty picking a topic, offer a short list of topics for them to select from, or ask them questions to stimulate their own thinking.

    Examples: "What did you do last weekend?"
    "What do like most about your job?"
    "What is your favorite sport?"

- You can use this activity as a follow-up to something the learners have done together: reading a story or a newspaper article, or taking a field trip, for example.

- As learners become more comfortable with the writing process, you may want to give them several opportunities to rethink and revise their writing—just as experienced writers do.

(Adapted from a presentation by Beverly Ann Chin.)

 Activity 53 Free Writing: Dialogue Journals

Purpose

To give learners an opportunity to use and appreciate writing as a form of communication; to correspond with another person in English through print

How

1. Ask each learner to bring a notebook to the next class.

2. In the class session, ask the learners to write something for you to read in their notebook. Tell them that they can choose whatever topic they want. For example, they can explain something to you, ask you a question, tell a joke, tell you what they did last weekend, describe a fond memory—anything.

3. Tell the learners not to worry whether their grammar or spelling is correct or whether their wording sounds funny. The important thing is that they write something that they want to write and that *they* want to share with *you*.

   By not having to focus on correctness, the learners will begin—often for the first time—to appreciate writing as a way to communicate their ideas to someone else and not just as another exercise that they do to learn how to write. And they may be more encouraged to use writing to meet their daily communication needs outside of the class.

4. Explain that you will not correct or change anything they write and that their writing will be confidential. No one except you will see it. When they have all finished writing for today, you will collect their notebooks, take the notebooks home, and write a response to each learner. Tell them that this is the first of many written exchanges you will be having with them in the form of a dialogue journal. Tell them that next time they will do their writing on their own at home.

By keeping the learners' writing confidential and not making any corrections to it, you are freeing the learners from worrying about being right or wrong. You are allowing them to simply experience a private conversation between two people who are interested in communicating with each other.

5. Give the learners time to do their writing. Circulate around the room and give whatever help is needed. If a learner is having difficulty getting started, talk with him or her and ask questions to get the learner started. For example, you could suggest that the learner write about what he or she did the previous weekend. When the learners are done, collect the notebooks and take them home with you.

6. When you've read a journal entry, put the current date below the learner's entry and write your response. If the learner asked questions, try to answer them. If not, make comments "triggered" by what the learner wrote.

   By responding to what the learners write, you will help them understand that their ideas are worthwhile and meaningful. You will also help them gain a better sense of how to write for a specific audience—you!

7. Although you do *not* make any corrections to the learner's entry, you can model the correct English in what you choose to write yourself. Example:

   December 1
   Wishing to go home Cristmas.

   December 5
   I wish I could go home for Christmas, too.
   I haven't been home for Christmas in three
   years. When was the last time you were home?

8. Since your goal is to keep the dialogue going, you might want to end each of your entries with a question. This can make it easier for the learners to get started on their next entries. But explain to the learners that they do not have to limit themselves to answering your questions. They can also choose to write about an entirely different topic.

9. Continue this process through subsequent weeks, except have the learners take their journals home to write in. They will write in class only in the session in which you first introduce the dialogue journals. You might want to require that the learner write one entry each week. You'll probably find that learners are initially reluctant to do much writing: They are still trying to figure out what the assignment "really" is. Eventually, they will relax and begin to communicate with you in a true dialogue.

Suggestions

- Use printing when you write in the journals—especially when you are working with beginning learners.

- Be patient. With time, learners will become more communicative, and their writing will be more varied, more complex, and more creative.

- Dialogue journals are not meant to replace other writing activities you do with learners. They do, however, provide an enjoyable alternative to more traditional writing exercises.

Integrated Communication Activities

Some of the most effective ESL teaching activities are those that encourage the learners to communicate with others to complete a task. Integrated communication activities involve all four basic language skills: listening, speaking, reading, and writing. Learners work with the tutor or with each other on a task that requires them to think critically and to use their language skills. The focus is on the task at hand, not on the skills themselves.

Although the integrated communication activities described below are designed for beginning-level learners, they can be adapted for more advanced learners as well. In either case, learners need to have some facility in all four basic language skills in order to do the activities.

Information Grids

An information grid activity is interactive in nature. It involves learners in purposeful classroom communication which they can apply to practical tasks in the outside world. The grid itself is a learning aid in table form created by the tutor. The grid helps learners organize information on a specific topic.

Information grids are typically created around topics related to the learners' backgrounds and interests. One of the most common topics is personal information about the learners themselves. Learners will need to provide this kind of information when applying for a job, enrolling their children in school, or seeking medical assistance. In such situations, people are often required to provide this information on a specific form. Such forms seldom allow people to give answers in complete sentences as learners might have been practicing in class. For example, a job application form usually requires the applicant to briefly list previous jobs, employers, and reasons for leaving those jobs.

Information grids provide effective practice in listening and speaking. Learners answer the tutor's or teacher's questions and ask each other questions. They listen to conversations between the tutor or teacher and other learners. The learners also have the opportunity to practice their reading, writing, and critical-thinking skills as they work together to complete the grids.

Activity 54 Information Grids: Basic Steps

Purpose

To enable learners to communicate basic information about themselves and to request similar information from others, both orally and in writing

How

The steps below constitute the basic two-part teaching technique to use for most information grids.

Create the grid

1. Select a topic for the grid.

    Example: Things people ask each other when they first meet.

2. Select the column headings you want to use.

3. Create the grid on a chalkboard, overhead transparency, or sheet of flip chart paper so that all the learners can see it. In the left-hand column, write a number for each learner in the group. The example on p. 141 is set up for a group of six learners.

4. Select a learner. Write the learner's name on the first line as you repeat the name slowly and clearly. (Learners may be unfamiliar with names of people from other countries.)

5. Ask the learner questions to find out what information you should put in the remaining columns.

    Examples: "Where do you come from?"
    "How long have you been in the United States?"

6. Write the learner's responses on the grid. Read aloud what you have written.

7. Repeat this process with two other learners.

8. When you have completed the chart for the first three learners, select two other learners to work as partners. Ask one partner to interview the other using the same questions that you have been asking. ("Margaret, ask the same questions of Carlos, please.") Write the person's name and responses on the grid.

9. Ask the partners to reverse roles and repeat the interview process. Write the new name and responses on the grid.

10. Ask for a volunteer to interview a learner who hasn't yet been involved. Write the learner's name and responses on the grid.

    (If you have a large group of learners, do not create a grid that will include everyone. Limit it to five or six learners. You will be able to involve the rest of the learners in steps 12–14.)

Name	Homeland	How Long in United States	Married or Single	Number of Children
1. Miecko	Japan	6 months	M	1
2. Vincenzo	Italy	2 months	S	0
3. Dagoberto	Chile	1 year	M	3
4. Monisha	India	9 months	M	1
5. Diego	Mexico	2 years	S	0
6. Trang	Vietnam	1 year	S	0

11. Review the information on the grid, including each person's name. This is especially important for beginning-level learners and those who might have difficulty reading some of the words.

Ask questions about the grid

Once the grid has been completed, you can ask any number of questions that require the learners to read and understand the information shown on the grid.

12. Ask the learners some simple questions that can be answered directly from the information shown on the grid. Examples:

    "Who is from [Country]?"
    "How long has [Name] been in the United States?"
    "Is [Name] married?"
    "How many children does [Name] have?"
    "Who has the most children?"

Each time you ask a question, allow plenty of time before you call on someone to answer it. This ensures that all the learners will think about how to answer the question.

13. Select a learner to ask another learner a question based on the grid. Repeat this procedure, giving each learner a chance to ask and answer at least one question.

14. With more advanced learners, you can ask more difficult questions to help foster critical-thinking skills or require learners to work with more than one piece of information. You can then encourage the learners to make up similar questions to ask other members of the group. Examples:

"How many of the people in the grid are women?"
   (There is no gender category on the grid. Answering this question correctly calls for knowing which names are those of men and which are those of women. This is not always easy in an ESL class, since gender is not readily discernible from many names.)

"How many of these people are from Asia?"
   (Answering this question correctly requires knowledge of geography.)

"What year did [Name] come to this country?"
   (This question requires the learners to use subtraction.)

Suggestions

- When creating a grid for beginning learners, ask each learner the same question before moving on to the next question. For example, in the above grid, write the first learner's name and ask her where she is from. Then write the other learners' names in turn, asking each to answer the same question. Return to the first learner to ask how long she has been in the United States. Ask each of the other learners this question, and so on. When you are ready to have the learners try asking the questions, have each person ask only one question. For example, you can say, "Wong, ask Farah where he is from" rather than "Wong, ask Farah all these questions."

- When the learners are asking each other questions to create the grid, you can ask the learner who is answering the questions to write his or her answers on the grid. If the learner doesn't feel comfortable writing in front of the rest of the class, do the writing yourself. Or select a more advanced learner to do the writing. Later, as learners become more comfortable with the process, they can fill in the answers for themselves.

- To create a more interactive activity, select a topic and write the column headings and numbers on a piece of paper. Make a copy for each learner in the group. Have the learners complete their own grids by circulating around the classroom and interviewing each other. Before they begin, review the kinds of questions they will need to ask to complete their grids.

- In a multi-level ESL class, the more advanced learners can ask the lower-level learners questions based on the information in the grid.

- If the learners have begun to work on writing, ask each learner to use information from the completed grid to write sentences about other people in the group. ("Write a sentence about Marta and how long she has been in the United States.") If the learners have difficulty writing sentences by themselves, you can do the writing as they dictate the sentences. The learners can then copy these.

- You can use information grids to poll the learners about their likes and dislikes to help them see how they are similar and different. For example, list the learners' names down the left-hand side of the grid. List the names of various sports across the top as column headings *(Football, Baseball, Basketball, Soccer, Swimming).* Put a plus (+) or a minus (–) under each heading to show whether an individual learner likes or dislikes that sport.

- You can also use information grids as a pre-reading activity to help the learners see what they already know about the topic of the reading text or to introduce key vocabulary that will be used in it. For example, if the learners will be reading about different occupations, you might want to prepare them by creating a grid that can help them talk about their own jobs. Example:

Jobs					
Name	Occupation	Deal with Public?	Indoors or Outdoors?	Advanced Training?	How Long in Job?
1.					
2.					
3.					

Activity 55 Information Grids to Meet Real-Life Needs

Purpose

To prepare learners to provide information about themselves that will be required to meet specific real-life needs

How

Use the steps described in Activity #54 to help learners create and discuss grids that prepare them to handle specific real-life situations. The following is an example of this type of grid.

Example: Preparing for a doctor's appointment

Going to the Doctor				
Name	Age	Problem	How Long Had It?	Had It Before?
1.				
2.				
3.				
4.				
5.				
6.				

Activity 56

Information Grids to Review and Reinforce Specific Grammatical Structures or Vocabulary

Purpose

To reinforce specific grammatical structures or vocabulary and to generate conversation about how learners are alike or different

How

1. Use the steps described in Activity #54 to help learners create a grid that reinforces the grammar and vocabulary they are studying and to generate conversation. You can use almost any topic. The sample on p. 145 is for a group that has been discussing time, the use of the abbreviations *a.m.* and *p.m.,* and the use of the simple present tense ("I get up" vs. "I am getting up").

What Time do you . . . ?				
Name	Go to Bed	Get Up	Eat Breakfast	Leave for Work
1. Maria	10:00 p.m.	6:30 a.m.	yes	7:15 a.m.
2. Wong	11:00 p.m.	6:00 a.m.	yes	7:00 a.m.
3. Luis	11:30 p.m.	7:00 a.m.	no	8:00 a.m.
4. Ivan	9:00 a.m.	4:00 p.m.	yes	10:30 p.m.
5. Frieda	9:30 p.m.	6:00 a.m.	no	6:30 a.m.

2. Ask questions that learners can answer directly from the grid. Examples:

> "What time does Frieda go to bed?"
> "How many people get up at 6:00 a.m.?"
> "Who leaves for work at night?"
> "Who leaves for work last in the morning?"

3. Ask more difficult questions that require learners to manipulate the information in the grid. Examples:

> "Who gets more sleep, Luis or Maria?"
> "Who spends the least amount of time getting ready for work in the morning?"

Activity 57 Information Grids in One-to-One Tutoring

Suggestions

There are several ways to adapt information grids for use in a one-to-one learning situation:

- Use the same grid as the one shown on p. 141. On the left-hand side, list three names of people that the learner knows well, such as family members or friends. Then list three names of people that you know (preferably people who were not born in this country). Ask the learner the questions necessary to enable you to complete his or her part of the grid. Then complete your own part as you talk about the people you know. ("My friend Dagny is from Denmark. She has been in this country for 75 years.") When you complete the grid, ask questions such as the following:

"How long has my friend Dagny been in this country?"
"How many children does my sister have?"
"How many people are from Asia?"
"Who has been in this country longer—your sister Maria, or my friend Stefan?"

- Create a grid that lists something in the left-hand column other than people's names. An example might be a grid about transportation. The purpose of completing the grid might be to have the learner understand and practice using the words *often, sometimes, seldom,* and *never.*

How often do you use these?				
Type	Often	Sometimes	Seldom	Never
1. bicycle				
2. car				
3. bus				
4. subway				
5. train				
6. plane				

Teaching Adults: An ESL Resource Book

Information Gaps

Information gap activities require learners to use their English language skills to share information to complete a task—a true communicative task. The learners cannot complete the task with the information they have at the beginning of the activity.

During the activity, the learners interact to exchange information for a real purpose—which is exactly the way people use language in real life. The learners are not merely parroting phrases and sentences that the tutor says, nor are they asking questions to which they already know the answers. ("Maria, ask Wong what his name is and if he is studying English.") Instead, the learners are asking their own questions, giving commands, and giving and receiving *information that is new to them.*

An information gap activity is always used as a follow-up or practice activity and should not be used to introduce new material. Before beginning the activity, be sure that you have already introduced the vocabulary or grammatical structures that the learners will encounter. Try to build some kind of information gap into every review and reinforcement you do; virtually every activity in this book has one.

The activities below require learners to use listening, speaking, reading, and writing to fill information gaps. Some information gap activities may require only listening and speaking. For an example of one of these, see Activity #8.

Information Gap: Supermarket Ad

Activity 58

Purpose

To provide an opportunity for learners to practice using vocabulary related to grocery shopping

How

1. Collect supermarket ads that advertise a variety of different food products. You will need two copies of each ad. (If you don't have a second copy, you can make a photocopy.)

2. Make two copies of a shopping list with two columns. At the top of the first column, write the heading *Item.* At the top of the second column, write the heading *Price.* In the first column write the names of eight foods that are listed in the ad. Leave the price column blank. See the example at right.

Item	Price
orange juice	
bread	
apples	
chicken	
hot dogs	
tomatoes	
rice	
carrots	

Teaching Adults: An ESL Resource Book

3. On one copy of the ad, use a marker to black out the price of four items that are on the shopping list. On the second copy of the ad, black out the prices of the other four items that are on the shopping list.

4. Prepare one set of materials (two copies of an ad with different sets of prices blacked out and two copies of the related shopping list) for each pair of learners. Use a different ad for each pair. The ads should all contain some of the same food items, however.

5. Give the set of materials to each pair of learners. Ask each person to take one copy of the ad but not to show it to his or her partner.

6. Ask each learner to find in the ad the foods that appear in the shopping list. They should then fill in the shopping list with as many prices as possible. Explain that they need to include any special information related to the price. Examples: whether the orange juice price is for a 6- or 12-ounce can, whether the carrot price is for one pound or three pounds.

7. Explain that the learners will not be able to fill in all the prices by themselves. Tell them that they must ask their partner questions in order to fill in the remaining prices. (They cannot simply look at each other's ad.) The partner should give the price and any additional information necessary. Example:

    "How much is the chicken?"
    "The chicken is two dollars and nineteen cents a pound."

8. Give each pair four minutes to complete the activity.

9. When the learners have filled in all the prices on their shopping lists, select one person to read his or her shopping list aloud to the group (items and prices). Ask the other pairs to listen to see if they have any of the same items on their shopping lists.

10. Ask pairs who had the same items to tell the group whether their prices were the same or different.

Suggestions

- Ask each learner to go to his or her local supermarket, find the foods on the shopping lists used in this activity, and compare the prices charged by that market to the prices written on the shopping list. Or work with the group to create an entirely new shopping list. Ask each learner to copy this new list, take it to a local market, and write down how much the items cost there. They can then compare their findings at the next class.

- Use the activity to review food categories. For example, ask each learner to write the word *fruits* on a sheet of paper and then list all the fruits named in the ad.

Information Gap: Johari Windows

Purpose

To enable learners to use listening, speaking, reading, and writing to find out how the learners are alike and different

How

1. Divide the group into pairs. Designate one person in each pair as *A* and the other as *B*.

2. Create a "Johari Window" like the following on an 8½" x 11" piece of paper. Make one copy for each pair.

Both A and B	Only A
Only B	**Neither A nor B**

3. Tell the partners they must work together to complete the grid. Give them these instructions:

   "In the **top left-hand box** write three things you can *both* do."

   "In the **top right-hand box** write three things *A can do but B cannot do.*"

   "In the **bottom left-hand box** write three things that *B can do but A cannot do.*"

"In the **bottom right-hand box** write three things *neither* of you can do."

4. Tell the learners how much time they will have for completing this activity. The amount of time you specify can vary according to the learners' skill level.

5. When they finish, write the following on the board:

    I was surprised to learn that . . .

6. Call on a few of the learners to complete this sentence.

7. Ask for volunteers to tell the rest of the class what they learned about their partners.

Suggestions

- In a one-to-one situation, include yourself in the activity. You and the learner will work together to complete the grid.

- If the partners are still continuing their discussion after the allotted time, let the activity run longer— even if they have completed their chart. This activity is an effective conversation starter that often results in lively, animated discussions about the things that learners can and cannot do.

- Vary the activity by using different sentence beginnings:

    I have/don't have . . .
    I like/don't like . . .
    I am/am not . . .
    I have/have never . . .

(Adapted from Richard and Marjorie Baudains, *Alternatives: Games, Exercises and Conversations for the Language Classroom,* © 1990 by Longman Group Ltd. Used by permission.)

Other Integrated Communication Activities

Activity
60 Command Strips

Purpose

To engage the learners in an enjoyable activity that requires them to work together and to use the four basic language skills—speaking, listening, reading, and writing—to complete a task

How

1. Pre-teach any vocabulary needed for this activity.

2. Make a photocopy of the "Command Strips" on p. 154. Cut the 10 numbered strips apart.

3. On an 8½" x 11" piece of paper make five horizontal lines across the top and two circles below the lines. (See the example at right.) Make a copy for each learner.

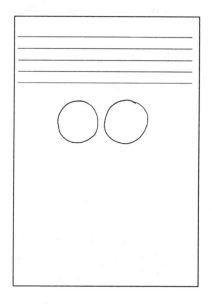

4. Give each learner one of the 10 command strips and a copy of the paper with the lines and circles.

   (Distribute all the strips. If there are fewer than 10 learners in the group, give some learners more than one strip. If there are more than 10 learners in the group, one or more learners will not receive a command strip.)

5. Explain that you will ask the learners to read their strips one at a time. Everyone will listen and then carry out the command.

6. Ask the learner who has strip #1 to read the strip aloud. ("On the first line, in the upper right-hand corner of the page, write the teacher's name.") Then ask everyone to follow the command using the paper with the lines.

7. Tell the learners to ask the reader to repeat the command if they didn't hear or understand it.

8. Repeat this process for each of the remaining nine commands. Call on the learners to read them in numerical order.

9. When the group has read and carried out all 10 commands, collect the original command strips. Each learner should now have a paper that looks something like the diagram at right.

10. Divide the learners into pairs.

11. Give each pair another blank piece of paper. Tell them to look

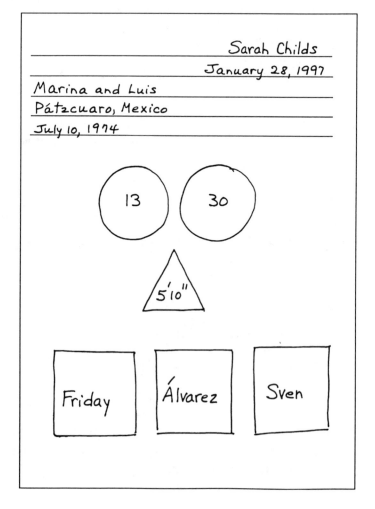

at what they wrote on their individual papers and then try to write all 10 of the original commands on the blank paper you just gave them. Tell the learners how much time they will have to complete this activity. The amount of time you specify will vary according to the learners' skill level.

12. If a pair of learners is having difficulty because they do not agree on a given command, give them any needed help. You may have to reread the command.

13. Select one pair of learners and ask them to read the commands that told what to put on the lines at the top of the page.

14. Select a second pair of learners and ask them to read the commands related to the circles and the triangle in the middle of the page.

15. Select a third pair of learners and ask them to read the commands related to the boxes at the bottom of the page.

Suggestions

• As a follow-up activity, ask each learner to create an entirely different set of commands. They can then either read these to a partner or use them with the whole class in an activity similar to the one you just did with them.

• In a one-to-one teaching situation, you will read all the commands to the learner. The learner then tries to write all 10 commands on the blank paper. Assist the learner as needed.

(Adapted from a presentation by Kevin Keating.)

Command Strips

1. On the first line, in the upper right-hand corner of the page, write the teacher's name.

2. On the next line, under the teacher's name, write today's date.

3. On the next line, at the left-hand side of the page, write your father's and mother's first names.

4. On the next line, under these names, write the city and country where you were born.

5. On the next line, below the city and country, write your date of birth.

6. Inside the first circle, write the number **13**. Inside the second circle, write the number **30**.

7. Draw a triangle below the circles. Inside the triangle, write your height.

8. Draw three large boxes across the bottom of the page. Inside the first box, write what day of the week it is today.

9. Inside the second box, write your last name.

10. Inside the third box, write the first name of the person next to you.

(for use in Activity #60)

"I'm a Banana. What Are You?"

Purposes

This activity combines speaking, listening, and reading and can be used for the following purposes:

- as a fun way to reinforce the correct English to use to approach people and ask them questions and to exchange information

- as a review of recently taught vocabulary

- as a "stand-up-and-reenergize" activity

- as a technique to divide a large group of learners into smaller groups

How

1. Decide how many categories of objects you want and what the categories will be. Examples: *fruits, cooking utensils, vegetables, clothing.* (If you are using the activity as a fun way to divide the learners into a specific number of small groups, use that number of categories.)

2. Make a list of items for each category. The total number of items needs to equal the number of learners in the group. (Each category should have approximately the same number of items.) Example (for a group of 16 learners):

Fruits:	banana, apple, pear, orange
Cooking utensils:	frying pan, spatula, egg beater, measuring cup
Vegetables:	carrot, cabbage, onion, potato
Clothing:	shoe, jacket, shirt, hat

3. Give each learner an index card on which you have written the name of one of these items. (Do not write the category names on these cards.)

4. Ask the learners to get up and walk around the room. As they approach other learners, they should say, "I'm a [item listed on their card]. What are you?" Their objective is to find all the other learners who belong in the same category as they do.

5. When the learners have found the others in their category, ask them to sit together and write a list of all the items they can think of in that category. Give them three or four minutes for this part of the activity.

6. When the time is up, ask a member of each group to tell what category the group members belong to and to read aloud the items they wrote on their list.

Suggestion

Give learners extra time to continue their conversations if they seem interested in what they are discussing. This sort of "free" conversation should always be encouraged.

Pulling It All Together: Lesson Planning

A lesson plan helps you decide in advance what skills to work on and what materials and activities to use during the lesson. It provides you with a structure for the lesson—showing not only what you and the learners will do, but also for how long and in what order. In addition, the lesson plan becomes a permanent record of what you have taught. It is a handy reference when you are designing future lessons.

Two Ingredients of a Lesson Plan

In creating a lesson plan, you will usually need to allow time in the lesson for both of the following:

1. Work in the core instructional materials or series

   A published ESL instructional series such as *LifePrints* or the *Laubach Way to English* series (see Appendix A) helps you to teach the basic English skills that *all* ESL learners must develop, whatever their individual needs or interests. Examples: the ability to greet someone, to ask for directions, to use a telephone book. Using a well-designed instructional series will also help you feel more confident: you won't have to worry about missing any key skills. It will also save you time since you won't have to create all the activities from scratch.

2. Activities designed to meet the learners' individual needs

   In this part of the lesson, you will be addressing the *individual* needs that you identified when you did the learners' needs assessments (see pp. 33–34). Examples:

   - for learners in a workplace setting: learning to read the words on a parts inventory

   - for learners who are parents of young children: learning how to communicate with their children's teachers

- for learners who depend on public transportation: learning how to call for information about bus schedules

Steps in Lesson Planning

To plan the part of the lesson that will address the learners' individual needs, simply ask the three questions *Who? What?* and *How?*

The following example is based on a tutor who is working in a one-to-one situation. If you are working with a group of learners, you should try to identify needs that are common to all or many of the learners. Sometimes you will choose to address a need that was identified by only one or two learners. When doing so, try to ensure that the discussion and practice will also be useful to the other learners. If a learner has a very specific or immediate need, set aside some time to work with that person after class.

Step 1: Ask *Who?*

The following learner profile was developed from information obtained during the initial needs assessment and from a very preliminary evaluation of the learner's English skills. It shows how one tutor answered *Who?* for the learner Song Chann.

Learner Profile: Song Chann

Approximate age:	early 20s
Homeland:	Cambodia
How long in United States:	one year
Family:	husband (housepainter) two daughters (2 and 4 years old)
Job in United States:	office cleaning (part time, evenings)
Work experience in homeland:	seamstress
Education:	high school graduate (Cambodia)
Personal interests:	sewing, singing, painting
Goal:	to become a nurse
Reasons for learning English:	• to communicate with English-speaking coworkers at her current cleaning job
	• to enter nursing school
English skills:	• studied English in Cambodia but speaks only a little
	• understands some English if spoken slowly

You can use the information in the profile to develop learning objectives. Learning objectives tell what the learner will learn or be able to do by the end of the lesson (or several lessons). The objectives should be specific and focused rather than general. They should be written in such a way that it will be easy to tell when the learner has met the objective. Examples of specific objectives for Song Chann might include the following:

1. She will be able to ask a stranger for directions.

2. She will learn vocabulary related to office cleaning.

3. She will be able to tell someone about the members of her family.

When developing learning objectives, think about what happened in previous lessons if applicable. For example, did the learner share her frustration at not being able to understand someone on the telephone? Did the learner start to tell you about a special dish she likes to prepare but then stopped because she didn't know the English names of the ingredients? Think of such unplanned-for events as "teachable moments," and take advantage of them whenever they happen—even if you have to set aside something else that you had planned to do during the lesson. These are golden opportunities to teach something that the learner considers important. If appropriate, you can develop objectives for future lessons that build on this learning.

Step 2: Ask *What?*

For each objective ask *What?:* "What topics and language skills do we need to address to meet this objective?"

For example, Song Chann's tutor might choose the topic of "Basic Cleaning Tools" to address the second objective. The tutor will then identify the vocabulary *(mop, broom, dust cloth)* and language skills (asking questions such as *May I have the _____?* and *Where is the _____?)* that Song Chann will work on.

Step 3: Ask *How?*

Ask yourself, "How will I teach these skills?" This will help you select the appropriate materials and activities for teaching the new vocabulary and language skills.

After you answer these three questions, you will be able to create a lesson plan outline like the one on p. 160.

Lesson Plan Outline: Song Chann

Learning objective:	Song Chann will be able to communicate about the standard cleaning supplies she uses at work.
Topic:	basic cleaning tools
Language skills:	vocabulary: *mop, broom, dust cloth*
	questions: *May I have the _____?*
	Where is the _____?
Activities:	vocabulary: Total Physical Response
	questions: dialogue and role play
	practice using questions
Materials:	objects (or pictures of): mop, broom, dust cloth
	picture of typical office interior from *The New Oxford Picture Dictionary*

Step 4: Write the Lesson Plan

The next step is to create the complete lesson plan that shows exactly what the learner will do. You can use the "Lesson Plan Activity Sheet" form on p. 164 to do this. See pp. 162–163 for a sample of a lesson plan that the tutor used with Song Chann after they had met together several times.

As you look at the completed lesson plan, note the following.

Free conversation

Try to start each lesson with a few minutes of free conversation. This gives the learner an opportunity to ease into English during the first few minutes of the session without having to worry about learning anything new. It allows the learner to use English to communicate, gaining valuable practice in choosing what he or she wants to say in an informal social situation. Do not correct the learner's errors during free conversation.

Try to end your lessons with free conversation as well. To get the learner started, you might ask what he or she plans to do during the coming week.

Review

Always review what you taught in previous lessons. Recycling information is essential in language acquisition. You might choose to review a specific segment of a previous lesson or reuse vocabulary or grammatical structures in new activities.

Notes

Take careful notes. You can use the "Notes" section on the "Lesson Plan Activity Sheets" to record

- what you actually covered (You might not always be able to carry out everything you included in the lesson plan. That's fine, since you should always take the time to respond to unexpected questions or needs that arise from the learner during the lesson.)
- unplanned-for things that came up during a lesson
- ideas for topics or activities to include in the next lesson(s)

Variety

Use a variety of activities in the lesson. In the sample lesson plan for Song Chann, the tutor begins with a TPR activity to teach the names of cleaning equipment. The tutor then teaches a dialogue using questions about the location of this equipment. In a follow-up role play, Song Chann has an opportunity to use other English she knows to ask similar questions or to give the information to others. Song Chann then spends some time working on basic skills in the two instructional series the tutor has selected.

Reassessment

Periodically include time for reassessment of the learner's interests, goals, and language skills.

Lesson Plan Activity Sheet

Learner _Song Chann_
Date _November 8_
Length of lesson _90 minutes_

	Activity	Materials	Time	Notes
1.	**Free conversation**		5 min.	
2.	**Questions to review previous lesson** "What is May doing?" "Who do you send packages to?" "What is the name of the city?" (also state and country)	picture from p. 30 of *LifePrints* Level 1 Student Book	5 min.	
3.	**Cleaning the office** Total Physical Response	mop dust cloth broom picture of office (*The New Oxford Picture Dictionary*)	5 min.	
4.	**Teach questions** "Where is the _____?" "May I have the _____?"	same as #3 above	10 min.	
5.	**Dialogue and role play** supply room	Dialogue: A: Excuse me, please. B: Yes? A: Where is the supply room? B: Just down the hall. A: Can I get a broom there? B: Yeah, I think so. A: Thank you.	10 min.	

Lesson Plan Activity Sheet (continued)

Learner _Song Chann_

Date _November 8_

Length of lesson _90 minutes_

Activity	Materials	Time	Notes
6. **_LifePrints_ series** "Warm-up" days of the week postal vocabulary "Presentation"	_LifePrints_ Level 1: Student Book, p. 31 Teacher's Edition, p. 65 Props: calendar, stamps, package, postcard, letter	15 min.	
7. **Create an LEA Story**	(based on picture on p. 31 of _LifePrints_ Level 1 Student Book)	15 min.	
8. **Reading and Writing: _LWE_** review chart review first half of story read second half of story "Listen and Write"	_Laubach Way to English:_ _Skill Book 2,_ Lesson 7, pp. 32–34 _ESOL Teacher's Manual for_ _Skill Book 2,_ pp. 147–149	20 min.	
9. **Free Conversation**		5 min.	

Lesson Plan Activity Sheet

Learner _____

Date _____

Length of lesson _____

Activity	Materials	Time	Notes

Teaching Adults: An ESL Resource Book

New Readers Press Publications

The items listed below are samples of the materials available from New Readers Press. To obtain a current catalog, contact NRP at (800) 448-8878.

ESL Core Instructional Series

LifePrints

This three-level core instructional series helps learners develop language skills and cultural understanding through a wide variety of communicative activities including interviews, listening tasks, role plays, language experience stories, and games. The emphasis is on activities that integrate the language skills (listening, speaking, reading, writing), math, and authentic language in real-world contexts.

The three levels of *LifePrints* are low-beginning, high-beginning, and low-intermediate. Each level has a student book, an audiotape, a teacher's edition, and a teacher's resource file that contains a variety of supplemental activities. Assessment books contain achievement tests and informal assessment activities corresponding to each level of the series.

Laubach Way to English

This three-level ESL series is based on the *Laubach Way to Reading* series and provides instruction in basic speaking, listening, reading, and writing skills. The teacher's manuals provide guidance on how to teach oral skills through dialogue, vocabulary, structure focus, and pronunciation activities. They also contain instructions for teaching learners to read and write using the *LWR* skill books.

The components for each of the three levels of *LWE* are: a teacher's manual, a student skill book, an illustrations book, a workbook, a correlated reader with stories using the vocabulary and sentence structures taught in that level, a checkup booklet, and a diploma. Read-along tapes are also available for the skill books and correlated readers.

Oral Skills Development

The New Oxford Picture Dictionary

The dictionary is a highly illustrated reference tool for ESL learners who want to expand their English vocabulary. Bilingual dictionaries are also available in English plus one of the following languages: Cambodian, Chinese, Japanese, Korean, Polish, Russian, Spanish, and Vietnamese.

101 American English Idioms

This collection of American idioms and colloquialisms is organized according to topics and presented with humorous caricatures followed by dialogues or narratives to convey the meaning. The teacher's manual and resource book contains discussion questions, exercises, word games, and many reproducible activities. Author: Harry Collis.

Basic Grammar in Use

This book provides high-beginning and low-intermediate ESL learners with extra help in learning American English grammar. Grammatical structures and examples in natural language are presented along with exercises to reinforce understanding of the grammar points. The book can be used as a teaching text for grammar, a self-study guide, or a reference resource. Author: Raymond Murphy.

Clear Speech

This innovative pronunciation text places emphasis on the rhythm, stress, and intonation of English. Learner activities are placed in meaningful contexts to allow carryover to improved pronunciation outside of the ESL session. There is a student book of exercises and activities and a teacher's guide that explains the activities and provides additional ideas for working on improved pronunciation. Author: Judy Gilbert.

Survival English

Speaking of Survival

This book helps learners prepare for real-world situations such as banking, shopping, housing, auto repair, and medical emergencies. Conversations in each unit are prompted by a color photograph. Oral and written exercises reinforce vocabulary and structures associated with that topic. An audiocassette is also available that includes the conversations, vocabulary, and reading selections in the book. Author: Daniel B. Freeman.

Teaching Adults: A Literacy Resource Book

This book, part of the *Training by Design* collection, was developed by Laubach Literacy Action especially for volunteer tutors working with native speakers of English. Many of the 69 suggested reading and writing activities can be easily adapted for ESL learners. Useful appendixes include a list of 300 frequently used words, a list of important social sight words, help for teaching phonics, and an extensive list of sample word patterns.

The Sounds of English

By understanding how speech sounds are made, you will be able to describe what a learner needs to do in order to pronounce the sounds correctly.

Consonant Sounds

The following chart indicates which parts of the speech mechanism are used to produce the English consonant sounds and how the sounds are produced.

Note that the letter in slashes // in the first column represents the sound—not the letter. This sound can often be spelled in different ways. It can also appear in different positions within a word. Examples of both of these are included in the second column.

The following codes are used in the third column to describe the sounds:

    v = voiced (vocal cords vibrate)
  un = unvoiced (vocal cords do not vibrate)
    c = continuant (sound can be continued as long as the speaker has breath)
    s = stop (sound cannot be continued)
    n = nasal (sound comes through the nose)

Consonant Sounds			
Sound	**As In**	**Code**	**How Sound Is Made**
/b/	**b**ird, kno**b**	v, s	Stop air with lips together; open with small puff of breath. Voiced equivalent of /p/.
/p/	**p**an, sna**p**	un, s	Stop air with lips together; open with a big puff of breath. Unvoiced equivalent of /b/.

Consonant sounds continued ▶

Sound	As In	Code	How Sound Is Made
/d/	**d**ish, roa**d**	v, s	Lips and teeth slightly parted. Stop air with tongue tip touching the roof of the mouth just behind the upper teeth. Tongue is dropped as breath is expelled. Voiced equivalent of /t/.
/t/	**t**ent, mel**t**, mi**tt**	un, s	Lips and teeth slightly parted. Stop air with tongue tip touching the roof of the mouth just behind the upper teeth. Tongue is dropped as breath is expelled. Unvoiced equivalent of /d/.
/v/	**v**alley, ha**v**e	v, c	Lower lip touching upper teeth lightly. Air passes between the lip and teeth. Voiced equivalent of /f/.
/f/	**f**ish, **ph**one, tou**gh**, sta**ff**	un, c	Lower lip touching upper teeth lightly. Air passes between the lip and teeth. Unvoiced equivalent of /v/.
/<u>th</u>/	**th**e, brea**th**e	v, c	Tongue touches both upper and lower teeth—may be slightly inserted between teeth. Air passes through the opening formed by tongue and upper teeth. Voiced equivalent of /th/.
/th/	**th**anks, four**th**	un, c	Tongue touches both upper and lower teeth—may be slightly inserted between teeth. Air passes through the opening formed by tongue and upper teeth. Unvoiced equivalent of /<u>th</u>/.
/z/	**z**ipper, qui**z**, hi**s**, teache**s**, kid**s**, fu**zz**	v, c	Teeth close but not touching. Tongue tip approaches roof of mouth just behind the upper teeth, making a narrow opening. Air streams through this opening. Voiced equivalent of /s/.
/s/	**s**nake, **c**ity, mi**c**e, bi**c**ycle, ba**ss**	un, c	Teeth close but not touching. Tongue tip approaches roof of mouth just behind the upper teeth, making a narrow opening. Air streams through this opening. Unvoiced equivalent of /z/.

Consonant sounds continued ▶

Sound	As In	Code	How Sound Is Made
/zh/	measure, television, fission, azure, regime	v, c	Lips forward and squared. Teeth close but not touching. Tongue tip close to middle of roof of mouth. Tongue sides are up, forming a groove. Air passes through the groove. Voiced equivalent of /sh/.
/sh/	**sh**op, bu**sh**, **Ch**icago, mi**ss**ion, cap**ti**on, **s**ure	un, c	Lips forward and squared. Teeth close but not touching. Tongue tip close to middle of roof of mouth. Tongue sides are up, forming a groove. Air passes through the groove. Unvoiced equivalent of /zh/.
/j/	**j**ump, **g**entle, fu**dge**	v, s + c	A combination of /d/ and /zh/. Lips forward. Start with tongue tip touching the roof of the mouth behind the teeth (in the position for making /d/). Stop the air, then release as a continuant. Voiced equivalent of /ch/.
/ch/	**ch**ildren, ki**tch**en, mu**ch**	un, s + c	A combination of /t/ and /sh/. Lips forward. Start with tongue tip touching the roof of the mouth behind the teeth (in the position for making /t/). Stop the air, then release as a continuant. Unvoiced equivalent of /j/.
/g/	**g**irl, le**g**	v, s	Tongue tip down. Back of tongue touching the roof of mouth to stop the flow of air. Back of tongue is dropped as breath is released. Voiced equivalent of /k/.
/k/	**k**it**ch**en, mar**k**, si**ck**, **c**up, **Ch**ris	un, s	Tongue tip down. Back of tongue touching the roof of mouth to stop the flow of air. Back of tongue is dropped as breath is released. Unvoiced equivalent of /g/.
/l/	**l**eg, ro**ll**, ba**bb**le	v, c	Tongue tip touches roof of mouth just behind the upper teeth. Air comes out along the side(s) of the tongue. This is a voiced sound.

Consonant sounds continued ▶

Teaching Adults: An ESL Resource Book

Sound	As In	Code	How Sound Is Made
/r/	river, wrap	v, c	Tongue tip up—near the front of the roof of the mouth, but not touching. Lips forward and squared. Air passes over the top of the tongue. This is a voiced sound.
/h/	hand, behind	un, c	Has no position of its own. Position the tongue for the vowel following it and give breath sound with no voicing.
/w/	woman, reward	v, c	Lips forward and rounded. Air passes through the opening. Tongue is in a neutral position. This is a voiced sound.
/y/	yells, use (/yooz/)	v, c	Lips relaxed, teeth close together. Middle of tongue moves toward roof of mouth without touching. Air passes over the top of the tongue. This is a voiced sound.
/m/	man, lemon, same	v, c, n	Lips together. Air passes through the nasal cavity instead of the mouth. This is a voiced sound.
/n/	neck, canal, fine, gnaw, knock, Ann	v, c, n	Lips and teeth slightly parted. Tongue tip touching roof of mouth just behind upper teeth. Air passes through nasal cavity instead of mouth. This is a voiced sound.
/ng/	ring	v, c, n	Lips open. Back of tongue touches back of roof of mouth. Air passes through the nasal cavity instead of the mouth. This is a voiced sound.
/hw/	whistle	un, c	Lips rounded in preparation for /w/ sound. Sound starts with breath as in production of /h/ sound and finishes as /w/. Note: Many English speakers do not use this sound.

Consonant sounds continued ▶

Sound	As In	Code	How Sound Is Made
Combination Sounds with /k/:			
/k/ + /w/	**qu**arter, ac**qu**aint	(un, s) + (v, c)	See /k/ and /w/. The two sounds are produced one after the other in combination. In written English *q* is always followed by *u* except for some foreign words such as *Qatar* and *Aqaba*. However, in these cases, the sound is /k/, not /k/ + /w/.
/k/ + /s/	bo**x**, loo**ks**, pic**ks**	(un, s) + (un, c)	See /k/ and /s/. The two sounds are produced one after the other in combination.

Vowel Sounds

All vowel sounds are voiced continuants. They can be described by

- where in the mouth the tongue forms a hump
- whether the lips are rounded or unrounded
- whether the muscles of the lips and tongue are tense (tightened slightly) or lax (relaxed)

The best way to describe how a vowel sound is made is to indicate the position of the tongue hump. The following chart shows where the tongue hump is positioned for each of the English vowel sounds.*

	Front	**Central**	**Back**
High	/ē/ beat /i/ bit		/oo/ boot /uu/ book
Mid	/ā/ bait /e/ bet	/er/ bird /u/ but	/ō/ boat /aw/ bought
Low	/a/ bat	/o/ pot	

*Some vowel classification systems include a symbol for the vowel sound in words like *few* or *use.* In this book the sound is not described separately. It is considered a combination of the consonant sound /y/ and the vowel sound /oo/.

Try the following suggestions if you (or the learners) have difficulty distinguishing between high/low, front/back, unrounded/rounded, or tense/lax vowels:

- Say the front vowels in order from high to low: /ē/, /i/, /ā/, /e/, /a/. Notice that your mouth opens wider as you move through the list. Also notice that the hump made by your tongue stays in a front position. Say the back vowels /oo/, /uu/, /ō/, /aw/. Notice that the hump stays in a back position.

- Say the two high sounds /ē/ and /oo/ several times. Notice that the tongue hump moves from the front of the mouth to the back of the mouth. Notice also that the lips are unrounded when you say /ē/ and rounded when you say /oo/. Try this with the two mid sounds /ā/ and /ō/.

- Say the two front sounds /ē/ and /i/ several times. Notice that the muscles of the lips move from being tense to being lax. Try this with the following pairs: /ā/ and /e/, and /oo/ and /uu/.

The next chart describes how each English vowel sound is produced—where the tongue hump is located and whether there is tenseness/laxness or unrounding/rounding during production of the sound.

Vowel Sounds			
Sound	**As In**	**Code**	**How Sound Is Made**
Front			
/ē/	beat, eel, we, Steve, key	v, c	high/front, tense, unrounded
/i/	bit, Lynn, if	v, c	lower high/front, lax, unrounded
/ā/	bait, rate, say	v, c	mid/front, tense, unrounded
/e/	bet, feather	v, c	lower mid/front, lax, unrounded
/a/	bat, after	v, c	low/front, lax, unrounded
Central			
/er/	bird, her, burn	v, c	mid/central, tense, lips are forward and almost squared
/u/	but, from, tough	v, c	lower mid/central, lax, unrounded. In an unstressed syllable, e.g., _a-bove,_ this sound is referred to as the "schwa" /ə/.
/o/	olive, pot, father	v, c	low/central, lax, unrounded

Vowel sounds continued ▶

Sound	As In	Code	How Sound Is Made
Back			
/oo/	boot, flute, blue, chew	v, c	high/back, tense, rounded
/uu/	book, bush, could	v, c	lower high/back, lax, rounded
/ō/	boat, hope, slow, go	v, c	mid/back, tense, rounded
/aw/	saw, bought, Paul, taught	v, c	lower mid/back, lax, rounded

A diphthong is a vowel sound that starts out as one vowel and moves to another vowel sound position.

Diphthongs			
Sound	**As In**	**Code**	**How Sound Is Made**
/ai/	ivory, I, five, night, tie	v, c	Starts out as /o/ (low/central) as in *pot* and moves to /i/ (lower high/front) as in *bit*
/oi/	boy, boil	v, c	Starts out as /ō/ (mid/back) as in *boat* and moves to /i/ (lower high/front) as in *bit*
/ou/	house, how	v, c	Starts out as /o/ (low/central) as in *pot* and moves to /uu/ (lower high/back) as in *book*

Two Skills Assessment Tools

Basic English Skills Test (BEST)

The oral skills section is individually administered and takes about 15 minutes. To simulate real-life listening and speaking tasks, it includes several questions for the learner to answer about him or herself as well as questions based on photographs, maps, and signs.

The literacy section can be administered individually or in a group and takes about one hour. This section is also based on real-life reading and writing tasks such as recognizing dates on a calendar, understanding food and clothing labels, or filling out an application form.

The *BEST* test includes two forms (B and C) for use in measuring a learner's progress.

Available from: Center for Applied Linguistics   New Readers Press
                   1118 22nd Street N.W.   Department TBDE
                   Washington, D.C. 20037   P.O. Box 888
                   (202) 429-9292   Syracuse, NY 13210-0888
                                                          (800) 448-8878

English As a Second Language Oral Assessment (ESLOA)

Designed especially for use in volunteer programs, this test is an oral assessment only. It can be used to determine a learner's entry-level skills or to evaluate a learner's progress.

The *ESLOA* assesses learners at four different levels. At each level, it suggests structures and survival topics that are appropriate for learners at that level.

Available from: Literacy Volunteers of America
                 5795 Widewaters Parkway
                 Syracuse, NY 13214
                 (315) 445-8000